DIVINE LAZINESS

The Art of Living Effortlessly

JEREMY COLE

Uncarved Block Publications

ISBN: 978-0-473-42668-2

divinelaziness.nz

Dedicated to Zen

who had mastered laziness

Contents

I WASN'T ALWAYS SO lazy. That came about gradually, riddance by riddance, as questions sent into deep places all came back telling me just to relax. But there's more to relaxing than just going limp, and this book explores how to ride one without falling off into the other.

When I was a child with way too much energy my mother had the good sense to enroll me in a six-week martial arts course that had set up in town, presumably in an attempt to siphon some of my more annoying intensity away from the family home. (Me being the third of four boys, I assume she had long since mastered this sort of cunning deflection.) That six-week course became a long love affair between me and kung fu. Although that particular style didn't impress upon me any specific principles, it did lay the groundwork that would lead me a few decades later to the study of wing chun, whose principles and practice have been so important in the evolution of divine laziness.

Thus grew the joy of cultivating physical abilities, and the recognition of how important it is to train diligently if one is to progress at a thing. And sounding a deeper note was the portion of the curriculum dedicated to the cultivation of chi, that mysterious life-force spoken of in the East. The practice of nurturing this energy and directing its flow awakened an inkling of the power of a focused mind, as well as the knowledge that there is more to the human being that meets the eye (or the scientist's microscope). Also, through contact with some truly exceptional martial artists grew an admiration of the beauty and ease exhibited by one who has mastered an art form.

One other treasure was granted to me through this avenue: the practice of bowing. Although frowned upon in workaday culture, the art of bowing, when done sincerely, accesses powerful qualities: honour, respect, humility. These are excellent guides in the venture of living at ease.

The years spent in the crucible of that training were a fine foundation upon which later development could rest, and did indeed serve to channel my energies into something more profitable than annoying my brothers.

By and by I found employment as a jeweller alongside one of my dearest friends, Paul. The two of us were under the guidance of Geoff, a masterful jeweller who became a cherished friend and mentor, and whose kind guidance turned out to be quite a watershed for me.

Besides jewellery, Geoff was also neck-deep in Buddhism, a path whose tenets and principles were beginning to find their way into my interest through the frequent conversations we two would have on the subject. Often would Geoff summon me to his workbench from where I was filing a ring or assembling silver chains to pose the question "Who is it that's doing the work anyway?" encouraging me to consider the ramifications of such an inquiry. Or he'd remind me of the maxim that I consider to be classic Geoff, and which I still recall frequently: "Don't do what others do, lad," he'd say, "Do what others don't do." It was moments like these that made of my time in that workshop a sort of golden age of learning and discovery that centered on the jeweller's art form but encompassed far more than that

This was a period of great development in the realm of craftsmanship and its attendant appreciation for the beauty inherent in art forms, and also in the opening of eyes. Several incidents during this time planted seeds that grew eventually into the shape of this book.

The first of these was a remark that my friend Paul made one day as he was demonstrating to me the finer points in the construction process of a ring he was working on (he was by this stage a fine jeweller; I, still an unskilled neophyte). During one of the steps in the process he impressed upon me the importance of doing it precisely and thoroughly, even though later stages of construction would effectively render this area hidden from view. "The quality of the final product depends upon how well each step in the process is done," he told me, advice that struck deeply and remains a touchstone to this day. For everything we do is a step we take in the process of constructing our lives, and the overall condition of that life depends on the quality of each part that goes into its composition, even if those parts are hidden from view. A lovingly crafted life is therefore its own reward, while a careless journey finds its own squalor as its destination.

A second incident, one that would redirect my life, was the gift to me of a book. This book spelled out to me some of the things that reside at the heart of Buddhism. It contained (aside from the teachings that would be so influential) a handwritten note attached to the inner cover that read: *"Geoff, Best wishes in the practice & Dhamma. Bhikkhu Vajiro."* This was Geoff's treasured personal copy, given to him by a well-revered monk, and he was passing it on to me! Everything changed after reading that book. It whipped the carpet out from under my feet, and although at times I'd look down and pretend I could still see patterns and threads, I knew in my heart that I was now standing on nothing.

Shortly thereafter a door that was swinging ajar was pushed open a little further when Geoff took me one morning to meet with a Buddhist monk. This was my first encounter with a monastic, and it happened to feature the very same monk that had penned that brief note in the cover of that carpet-stealing book. Who knows what I was expecting—perhaps some otherworldly being who was above mundane chit-chat with an simpleton like me—but I was lost for words while sitting before that venerable recluse. Nevertheless, conversation ensued despite my hangups and I was struck by how normal he was. Normal, but not usual, and that was another great teaching: the wise person lives normally, but in a non-usual way; in a way that is deliberate, considerate, optimised for maximum freedom and minimum harm.

Inevitably this thrust upon me the great adventure that is meditation. Although it was within a Buddhist context that I first encountered meditation, it is by no means an exclusively Buddhist practice; wisdom traditions from all cultures and at all times throughout history have as their basis some form of meditative technique. A chapter of this book is dedicated to outlining in general terms this fundamental catalyst for wisdom and freedom; it is a primary tool in the art of living effortlessly. To pass on advice that was passed on to me: if you do nothing else, find a good meditation teacher and practice sincerely.

Some time later, another of the world's great wisdom traditions came by, again in literary form. This time it was the Tao Te Ching —the principle text of the quintessentially Chinese tradition of Taoism—that appeared before me and broadcast its strange and excellent message. Immersed as I was at the time in the practice of kung fu, Taoism seemed a good compliment, both being reflections of traditional Chinese culture and thought. Also, it seemed to round out certain areas of understanding I was navigating my way through in my fledgling attempts at meditation.

The content of the Tao Te Ching was at once so incomprehensible and so obvious that my mind for a while simply fell over, stunned by the utter madness and profound good sense of it. The gist of it seems to be to allow nature to take its course and to avoid unnecessary tampering with that; happiness will then result. Needless to say, much of what makes up this book has been gleaned from that masterpiece.

There is a traditional Maori proverb, beautiful in its simplicity and powerful in its imagery: "Ka mura, ka muri," which translates as "Walking backwards into the future." Just as one who walks backwards cannot know the path ahead or its destination and has only the past as informant, I had no clue of what lay in store when shortly thereafter I relocated to the capital.

My new residence was a stone's throw (if you can throw a stone across a harbour and over the lip of a valley) from the Buddhist monastery that has provided a sanctuary for my heart and a nourishing garden for wisdom ever since. This monastery belongs to the Thai forest tradition of Theravada Buddhism (Theravada means "word of the elders") in the lineage of the great meditation master Ajahn Chah, who was instrumental in reviving the Thai forest tradition and distributing its teachings and practices to the West.

To have access to a place where those teachings and that way of life were being actively cultivated was a great boon. I can still recall vividly my first visit there one magical winter evening in '99 —the smell of the wooden architecture and the enchanting glow of dim lights through the hazy evening gloom, the air cold and thick with mystery as I entered the cloister and proceeded to the meditation hall. Within, the stillness was palpable and welcoming as I found a seat for the first of what was to be many audiences with the profound silence of that place.

The years since have installed this remarkable sanctuary in my life as a touchstone for sanity, a refuge where people still talk sense and live with dignity and poise in a world gone insane with carelessness and greed. It is lessons learned there—lessons in wise and harmless living, in the ease brought about through moral integrity—as well as the ongoing encouragement for deepening meditation practice that have taken root in the heart and blossomed, giving fragrance to this life and substance to this work on divine laziness.

As this fragrance permeated deeper I noticed a yearning for the fruits of my vocation to be something more meaningful than the baubles I was currently producing (I had found employment with a local jewellery manufacturer whose factory floor was a far cry from the artisan utopia I had grown up in at Geoff's; it did, however, contain a shining jewel in the form of Kate who has been my companion ever since). I longed to be of more benefit to others, and this led me to the study of homeopathy. I had read about this healing art some years earlier and been greatly impressed by the pragmatic and principles-based system of healing described. Enthused, I had consulted a homeopath about some health issues I was experiencing at the time and a curative result was obtained. So, as I stood at the threshold of a new direction in life homeopathy was a most conspicuous option. And as luck would have it there was a college of homeopathy just down the road. The time had come to learn something new, so that's what I did.

As an art form epitomising divine laziness, I had originally intended to devote a chapter of this book to homeopathy, outlining its principles and practice. For various reasons I decided against that idea, but it is worth pointing out two of its central principles here.

The principle of similars

The seminal observation that led to the discovery and systematization of homeopathy as a healing art in the late 18th century by the German physician Samuel Hahnemann was the principle of similars. In fact, the word homeopathy itself comes from the Greek *homoios* (similar) and *pathos* (suffering), meaning "similar suffering." His observation was that substances that can cause symptoms in a healthy person (ie, make them sick) can cure those same symptoms in a sick person (*similia similibus curentur* as he termed it; "let likes be cured by likes"). The entire philosophy and practice of homeopathy is based upon this tenet, a practice which aims at "going with" the prevailing conditions of an illness, applying "more of the same" with the administered medicine rather than opposing or "fighting against" the symptoms of the illness by using medicines that have an opposite effect (*contraria contrariis*, as Hahnemann would put it; "treating opposites with opposites").

What excited me about this "going with" approach was that it had the same flavour and easeful way of according with nature described in the Tao Te Ching and therefore seemed to indeed be the natural way of treating the sick. This non-resistance, this alignment with the shape and momentum of reality as it presents itself is the very heart and soul of divine laziness and the key which unlocks the door to a life of ease and non-abrasion.

The principle of the minimum dose

Equally crucial to homeopathy, the principle of the minimum dose seems to be a stumbling block for many when trying to comprehend this potent healing art. While in principle it is simple enough—the quantity of a therapeutic agent required to bring about a cure is the minimum necessary—it is the routine usage of *extremely* minute doses of medicine, indeed infinitesimally small, that so defies belief and closes otherwise open minds to this profound and pragmatic aspect of homeopathy. A shame really, for the mettle to continue one's exploration in the face of details that seem to contradict prior assumptions is the quality that has always guided great adventurers beyond the known to the unimagined. Regardless, this proposition of using the minimum necessary to achieve an outcome is the effortlessness that is central to divine laziness.

And so, as well as acquainting me with an effective healing art, the study of homeopathy also laid some keystones in the foundation of an edifice in the making. But that edifice was hungry for more, and I barely had time to savour what had just been tasted before another adventure pulled me out the door.

It was an impulse which sprang up suddenly, who knows from where. I hadn't practiced any martial arts for years—yoga had taken its place in meeting a need for physical training—yet I announced to Kate, out of the blue and with a rare crystal clarity, that I needed to learn wing chun kung fu. I knew next to nothing about this Chinese martial art beyond a cursory mention on a TV show I'd recently seen and a brief conversation with a friend who'd investigated it years earlier. However, something demanded that my hiatus from the martial arts had gone on long enough and that wing chun was to constitute my next adventure.

As luck (or fate) would have it there happened to be a genuine wing chun sifu teaching in town, so I tracked down the school and approached with my enquiry. The sifu (Chinese for "father;" a term of respect used when addressing one's teacher), turned out to be a composed and welcoming Chinese man in his late fifties, pleasant to talk to but serious on the matter of learning wing chun. "Why do you want to learn wing chun?" he asked, in response to which I mumbled something about hearing it was the most effective martial art, citing my previous involvement in kung fu as some sort of eligibility. "Well, unless you can commit to at least six months for seeing out the beginners' course to decide whether or not it's for you, and then at least five more years to learn the basics, you might as well forget it."

This was a refreshingly frank proposal in a world cheapened by shameless advertising and competitive sales pitches but, as I was to learn, typical of my sifu who is motivated strictly by a love of the art and never by financial gain. I agreed to such a commitment, he accepted my request to become his student and the meeting was over. It seems serendipity made one last appearance, as one of his strictly half-yearly intakes of new students was scheduled for two weeks hence.

And just like that my entry upon the path of wing chun had begun. I didn't know it at the time, but this path would combine several notes that I had been trying to hum into a single harmonious chord. Something about having these various concepts laid out in a way that could be approached physically and practiced tangibly brought them into sharper focus for me. Not only could I see them more clearly, but I could play with them and receive instant feedback for my efforts. For example, the concept of non-resistance had been a central theme for me, but it was only once I started exploring it through the wing chun training exercise of chi sau ("sticky hands") that I began to get a tangible feel for what non-resistance means; one's aptitude at chi sau is commensurate with one's ability not to meet force with force.

Resistance is futile, and using too much force leaves bruises all over the show.

Regardless of where we act, whether in the training halls of an art form or the rounds of everyday life, the physics are the same: when we push against life we only feel it pushing back. The art of living effortlessly asks us to give up that struggle and settle instead into life's current with an ease I've come to know as divine laziness.

This book is written for we who, weary of a lifestyle that demands constant doing, are ready to give up that struggle. It offers a way to unyoke from the compulsive drive to achieve, a way to fall into freedom instead. And if we are already trying to cultivate freedom, but find our efforts amounting to just more rocks in the backpack of things to get done, this book provides the means and the reasons to allow those efforts to be effortless and to bring about the ease that should be their reward.

Acknowledgements

I'D LIKE TO THANK the following people for their contributions to this book. My mother, father and brothers for the raw materials, which were soaked in love and goodness. Sifu Peter Yu for patiently showing me sensitivity and effortlessness, despite my persistent refusal to get it, and Simo, for making that possible. Peter Fernando for conspiring in the idea of divine laziness, for unflagging encouragement and feedback on the manuscript, but most of all for being my primary role model for living heartfully (I owe you far more than you realize, my friend; if I have anything that can be called wisdom it has come through knowing you). Robert Frazer for the initial suggestion to write this book, and for your diamond-like sincerity. Andrew Morrison and Jörg Otto, for your many examples of how men may live with integrity. Peter de Vocht, for the many conversations that helped me get clear on what I was writing (I must have bored you to tears, but you couldn't get away: you were usually stuck in a car with me). Kate, for keeping a home while I sat at a desk, and for constantly showing me what generosity looks like.

Countless others have contributed, directly and otherwise, to the manifestation of this work. My heartfelt gratitude belongs to you all and I bow down heartily to you.

Introduction

WHY DO TODAY WHAT can be put off until tomorrow?

So much life is spent trying to get it all done. Attending to matters that warrant attention is one thing, but the mania for keeping on top of it all—to stay in control, or at least to maintain its illusion—is a thorn in our side that makes even the easy-chair painful. Keeping busy is often mistaken for living life well, which is a shame because the two have nothing to do with each other.

In spending our efforts what matters is quality, not quantity, and that is determined largely by timeliness. Timely activity handles what ought to be handled; the rest can look after itself. If we can taste the difference between that which is ripe for the doing and that which belongs to tomorrow or never, then we can leave in the future that which doesn't really need to be done today. And we can leave uninhabited that which needn't or shouldn't be done at all.

Developing the nimbleness that knows when to move and when to stay still (and how to do both or neither) is the art of living effortlessly. And leaving undone deeds that would only cause harm is the noble and liberating idleness—the divine laziness—that lies at its heart.

A path that leads from a life choking on its own hyperactivity right into that heart may seem to be lengthy. But although it spans a landscape of peaks and deep flowing streams, the gist of it can be covered in seven propositional strides.

One: We do too much

Whatever the reason, the common approach to living can only be described as doing too much. We take up a day and stuff it till no space is showing. Notions of stopping are frowned at, and being anxious to get things done is somehow seen as not only normal, but noble. We nurture a host of worries that ferment in our guts while we feed them our repose. Everything gets sore dancing to the beat of their sleepless drums.

On and on we drive ourselves, whipped by a compulsion to progress at all costs and with little regard for consequences as we endlessly fiddle with how a thing is or force it to be something else. We do it en masse as a species, believing that will solve every problem, and we treat our singular lives no less mercilessly.

A look around shows the face of anxiety peopling our streets and filling the screens that bring us the world, and with nose to the grindstone day and night it's no wonder that face looks so harrowed. As we work our nerves to the bone the strident voice of perpetual industry pesters our ears. The simple silence of going nowhere is lost in the din, and with it our birthright of being nobody doing nothing.

Two: Much of that doing is needless or detrimental

Maybe most of that hustle and bustle is not needed at all and gives nothing of value while sucking the marrow from us. Meaningless doing does a fine job of drowning the voice of silence that whispers, just out of earshot, things we'd rather not hear. But it's also a thief that pilfers our life, day by day, while leaving us fistfuls of nothing as payment.

So much of our time is spent trying to get ducks in a row. But the thing about ducks is they don't stay in rows. They waddle and wander about and they fly away. We're better off smiling to see them all over the show; to insist they be otherwise is to fill our lives with a row of dead ducks, and quacks are much nicer than the smell of decay.

Even our doings which are useful could probably be a lot leaner. We tend to use too much effort when acting and throw in far more than required, thrashing a thing that may only need a slight touch. Overexertion is unable to feel how much is enough and fritters away precious zeal that could be better utilized where it is actually needed.

Worse than that, much of our ill-considered activity bruises our world, inside and out. As our surroundings bear the brunt of our neanderthal fists, the delicate balance of our inner landscape gets crushed in the clenching of those fists. But we can't seem to leave things alone. A more deft and delicate hand is called for.

Three: There is a way that does the least while accomplishing the most

We don't have to be sentenced to work ourselves into a frenzy or fiddle and force ourselves out of our minds. There is a way to live free of that drudgery, a way that aligns with how nature moves.

It has been said that nature does nothing yet nothing is left undone. The natural way is efficiency and ease. It shuns the path of resistance, flowing instead down the arteries of effortlessness. In following this way, where there is movement we go along with it and ride in the current (as long as the course is a favourable one); then all that is needed is steering. And if there is nothing to do we simply do nothing and stay where we are.

This way is called divine laziness because it evades movement that damages welfare. Feeling acutely the flavour of every now, it tastes what is needed and pours itself into that, but—knowing well that every act is a cause that has an effect—leaves undone deeds that would only bring ruin.

Four: Walking this way is the art of living effortlessly

If we are to leave undone ruinous deeds we must first be able to see them for what they are. We can't know the future but we can learn to feel the results of our actions right here within us; we can notice too their effects in the world around us.

The backbone of the art of living effortlessly is the ability to discern what is to be done. That ability grows as we see more clearly the cause-and-effect nature of all that we do. Seeing how much of our doing is needless we can slacken our grip on it, letting the deadwood fall by the wayside. And knowing which actions spit curses into our future and which ones grow arms to embrace us, we can choose to stop planting disasters and instead build ourselves a real home.

Touching our world with a light and benevolent hand allows us to listen to it, rather than just trying to push it around. As we listen more deeply we hear the needs of each occasion and learn to respond with just the right touch, no more and no less than is asked for. The shape and nuances of every moment tell us the secret of how to align with them, and if and when it be time to use a heavier hand. That delicate voice is the sound of divine laziness, and with it in our ear we are guided well down the path of effortless living.

Five: This way is paved with sensitivity and effortlessness

Principles define and give shape to an art form; they are its bones and its blood. Those who seek to embody an art form do so by according with its principles. The art of living effortlessly rests upon two of them: sensitivity and effortlessness. These we must plant in our lives and nurture if we are to unbind the heart of divine laziness.

Sensitivity is the ability to feel the shape and nuances of a moment, to sense how and where it is flowing. It tells the mood of a room when we enter, or reads the tone of a conversation and offers the right things to say; it lets us know whether to act or do nothing at all. A baseline of this sensitivity in instilled in us through the process of living our lives, but sensing the fine inner workings of an instant asks of us something more (or is it something less?): it asks us to reach far deeper and touch the needs of each and every moment, that we may respond with effortless potency.

Effortlessness wastes not a drop of energy on futile resistance. As sensitivity develops we find ourselves pushing less against the world and ourselves, feeling how tedious pushing can be. Giving that up we accord instead with the flow of right now and simply go with it, adding something only where needed. Yes, we may need to steer things onto a more favourable track—as directed by our sensitivity—but often nothing needs doing at all.

Although sensitivity and effortlessness take the stage as defining principles of divine laziness, they are seen (if we look) to underpin any genuine art form. Training within an art form is always aimed at developing sensitivity to its tools and techniques, and the more skillful we become the less effort we waste on poor execution. We see this embodied by artists in every arena: the more sensitive the touch, the more effortless the performance and the more beautiful the result.

The crafting of our lives needs no less of a skillful touch, and although we may wish, like Michelangelo, to bring forth sublime images of life from inanimate stone, we cannot just pick up a chisel and hope to hack out a depiction of David while we are no more sensitive than the rock we are defacing. This way is an art, and it only takes form within a crucible of training.

Six: Imbuing a life with those principles takes training

Training sharpens the tools and techniques of an art form and deepens our embodiment of its principles. Having as its training ground each and every now, the art of living effortlessly uses this moment to develop sensitivity; that sensitivity grows in us the light and sure touch of effortlessness; and that effortlessness renders our training ever more efficient.

An assembly of rules always presides over training. Rules throw up walls around our conduct: walls that keep us from falling off cliffs; walls that limit our actions to those that are fertile so our training may bear fruit. Although they are strict those walls are not cold and severe; in fact they are an embrace. And, somewhat paradoxically, it is only through surrendering to that embrace— even though at times it may squeeze the comfort out of us—that freedom to act with artistry can develop.

Three realms of action—those of body, speech and mind—must feel the embrace of our training if we are to give them the sheen of freedom and ease. The first two, actions of body and speech, are checked and refined through adherence to moral guidelines. The third—the mind—is polished through meditative habits that temper and steer its activity. When these three are moving in harmony they may indeed start to shine.

Seven: The light at the end of the training is freedom and ease

Through steadfast cultivation of our art form we may come to a place where the rails of training run out and the ground gives way to a plunge into open space. This is the freefall of mastery, where the rules that govern our actions no longer apply and the subtle cues of each moment take their place as guides. Feathered with sensitivity, mastery's wings effortlessly carry us by catching the wind. Trusting ourselves to those wings we give up all hope of forcing ourselves to be anything other than this or go anywhere else. That is freedom and that is ease. And right there is divine laziness, the heart and goal of the art of living effortlessly.

And this is the way. This is the path leading out of the fray, and those who are ready to leave can follow it home. This way is nothing new. It has been walked and commended through the centuries by those far more qualified than I to speak of its merits, and venerable traditions have issued forth as a result. With freedom and ease at their source, these are the streams that flow as lifeblood through this book. Chief among them are the time-worthy arks of Buddhism and Taoism, but various others are drawn in their wake. And riding upon them and steering them stands the traditional martial art of wing chun, navigating with a disarmingly gentle touch.

Diverse as these are in their accents, when held just so they are heard to be singing the same alchemical song, soft as a feather and sharp as a thunderbolt. That song is divine laziness, and the singing of it is the art of living effortlessly. It's a chorus worth adding a voice to.

Chapter One

Overdoing

IT SEEMS WE ARE a species addicted to doing. A never-ending project sets our hearts on distant horizons while we stumble over where we are to get there. Recently some scientists agreed there is water on Mars, and declared that within a few decades we'll have colonized that enigmatic red orb. They say this is progress. Maybe it is. There's no denying the appeal of exotic planets, but the truth is we're already on one and it's incredibly majestic despite our determination to ravage it. And yet we expend astronomical amounts of energy trying to get to a place that will not even sustain human life. Some would say those efforts would be better spent elsewhere. Or not spent at all. But progress is progress, and if it's happening it must be good, right?

Must we do a thing just because it is there to be done? Or can we spend our actions more wisely? When we look we can see that all our activities fall under one of three categories: those that produce beneficial outcomes, those that are useless, and those that bring ruin. Some of our labours do indeed fly the first banner; they are useful, and leave both the doer and the done-to better off. This is the "progress" we like to congratulate ourselves on; the improvements we have wrought in our world through our ingenuity, our compassion, our industriousness. The widespread installation of educational and medical facilities across our planet; the development of art forms that uplift and inspire; the eradication of mortal yet easily avoidable diseases; with these as a gauge, yes, there has been progress.

Be that as it may, much of our activity probably falls short of this excellent standard, sliding instead into the other two classes. Either our actions are pointless and inefficient, fruitless eddies of habit or anxiety that sap our energy and make fools of our intentions while producing little of value in return. Or they are actually harmful—to the people and systems around us and, more directly, to ourselves. We will explore later the relationship of intention to action, and how the former determines the outcome of the latter. For now we can simply note how the mere fact that we *can* do a thing by no means implies that we *should*. And we can cast a somewhat mistrustful eye over a worldwide craze for keeping busy.

The great project

Some years ago I moved from my hometown to the capital and the contrast made the background hum of industry easy to hear. It sounded like hurry, that hum, and replies to the question "How are you?" all seemed to contain the word "busy" (often delivered as if that were somehow a good thing). Walking beneath acres of high-rise office blocks overflowing with people at desks I wondered what they were up to in there. And I wondered if it even needed to be done.

There are so many of us—billions of us—pouring constant effort into some mysterious, gargantuan project. What are we actually doing? Pulled from our beds by alarm clocks and coffee we run to arrive on time and in tune for the job, grateful to be a cog in this glorious machine. It's building something, this machine (and it's coughing black smoke as it does so), but the master plans don't exist and the project is running wild. Is there a goal or end in sight? Where is the finish line that tells us the job is done and it's time for a rest?

Sure, we (mostly) manage to put food on our tables, and (maybe) collect a few trinkets and toys along the way. But that's a meager reward for the efforts of an inexhaustible workforce toiling around the clock, day in, day out, year in, year out, endlessly. An engine of such awesome magnitude drawn onward by a clear and definite goal must surely be capable of anything. But it looks like there is no clear goal. Not really. Just adherence to business for business' sake and a desperate sprint lest we fly off the back of the treadmill for daring to stop. So day after day we grease the gears for one more spin around the track.

Though it is greedy and fat and shouts from every corner this perpetual campaign of progress seems to go unnoticed, so intrinsic it is to society. It's just a basic shared assumption that we must advance at all costs, as if existence itself were some sort of calamity in need of continuous repair or improvement. As if the way it is just now is untenable, and the prospect of simply leaving it alone is preposterous.

Of course, at times when the situation *is* untenable a little intervention is a fine plan. The ability to perceive a problem and effectively address it to the benefit of all involved is something to applaud. Our capacity to step in and extend a helping hand to our fellow beings, allowing them too to prosper from our experience or affluence, is satisfying, edifying. In such situations happiness and well-being spring from the things we do; to sit on our hands would be a shame.

So in raising an eyebrow at the heavy-handed use of industry it isn't doing per se that is eyed with suspicion. Living involves doing, of course. It's the compulsive drive to *overdo*, the tendency towards hyperactivity and chronic meddling that hounds us day and night and allows not a moment of rest. Doing when nothing needs doing, fiddling when things would be better left alone; these are the culprits in the theft of our quietude. As the old adage says: if it ain't broke, don't fix it. Leave well enough alone. The ceaseless drive to make everything better and faster and shinier—whatever the cost—is a madness that robs us of our most valuable birthright: the capacity to simply be.

We learn this madness young. Most of us are taught we must strive to excel at a limited bandwidth of activities: sports (the popular ones, not the weird ones), academic excellence (for those who are no good at the sports), financial shrewdness (if you missed out on the other two) and not many others. We are taught that happiness follows on the heels of these things. We're taught some other things too: like how we must never give up; that quitting is somehow the most pernicious of sins; that if we're not useful we're also not valuable. And we're taught it is definitely not okay to relax and just be as we are.

But what if we do quit? What if we give up? What if we relax and let it all be as it already is? Cease to uphold these societal taboos and perhaps they'll be seen for the murderers of ease that they are. Perhaps we'll see it's all lies, for happiness is independent of precarious conditions like success and achievement, and is in fact the substratum of our being. Happiness is our natural state and is always and only singing its song, but such tender strains are inaudible over the ruckus of striving. Of course, no one is deliberately trying to trick us into struggling our lives away so that we are unable to hear our own hearts. These ideologies are simply passed on, generation after well-meaning generation, as seemingly obvious and obviously unavoidable features of life.

Who knows when this started, or how. Maybe it's just how we are. But it seems we just keep getting better at running this fever of overdoing. We have furnished ourselves with more opportunities than ever before to stuff every second with an avalanche of clamouring distractions. We leave scant—if any—moments clear and unseasoned enough to taste the underlying flavour of simply being alive. Even that very idea—feeling alive—is conceived of as somehow resulting from *doing* something. Get famous, get rich, get everything you want; that's living. Jump from a plane or go running with bulls in Pamplona; that's the way to feel alive. Ever more ardently do we strive to elicit, by hook or by crook, our quota of elusive happiness.

Life has never been more convenient than now (at least for the fortunate among us): hot water at the touch of a button; larders bursting with surplus supplies; devices for instant communication whenever we wish. You'd think with all the time thus liberated we'd have relaxation and ease down to a fine art, yet more than ever our lives choke on a scramble of purposeless doing. On top of this, certain pathways traditionally signposting the way out of all of this—like the practices of yoga or mindfulness, for example—seem somehow to have been re-purposed by some[1] as yet further projects of "self-improvement."

The tendency to see everything as somehow flawed and in need of renovation is troublesome enough, but there's something else too: we have now at our disposal technologies with the power to cause destruction and horror on a scale previously reserved for extinction events. In light of this it seems worth exploring ways to relax the compulsive drive to improve things before we improve ourselves right out of existence along with any other species unlucky enough to be stuck here with us.

Swallowing flies

Although we can pride ourselves on our problem-solving abilities, there are times when our attempts at bettering a situation leave us worse off than if we'd left it alone. We see what we perceive to be a problem and we put in our corrective oar to steer the situation in what we assume is a better direction. Sometimes we actually do change things for the better, and everyone lives happily ever after. Great. But often we stack complications on top of each other, piling up problems that get more and more difficult to solve.

I remember from my childhood a song that told a delightfully absurd cautionary tale. Accompanied by cartoon illustrations, it described a strange old woman with an odd appetite, whose strategy for dealing with problems was throwing bigger ones at them.

> There was an old lady who swallowed a fly,
> I don't know why she swallowed the fly,
> Perhaps she'll die.
>
> There was an old lady who swallowed a spider,
> That wriggled and jiggled and tickled inside her.
> She swallowed the spider to catch the fly,
> I don't know why she swallowed the fly,
> Perhaps she'll die.
>
> There was an old lady who swallowed a bird,
> How absurd to swallow a bird!
> She swallowed the bird to catch the spider
> That wriggled and jiggled and tickled inside her.
> She swallowed the spider to catch the fly,
> I don't know why she swallowed the fly,
> Perhaps she'll die.

The verses go on to describe her progressively more outrageous attempts at rectifying these dietary errors—she swallows a cat to catch the bird, she swallows a dog to catch the cat, a goat to catch the dog, a cow (I don't know how she swallowed the cow) to catch the goat—until finally:

> There was an old lady who swallowed a horse.
> She's dead of course.

Whatever drives our overdoing is like that. Something occurs, perhaps not something monstrous, maybe just a fly. Chances are it would be just fine if we left it alone but we don't. Or we can't. We swallow a spider hoping that will sort it out. Soon enough, though, that wriggling inside becomes too unsettling so in goes the bird. And so on. Like using more oil to wash oil from a shirt, then yet more oil to wash *that* oil out, this strategy of addressing mistakes with bigger ones can only lead to disaster, each stage of the process making things worse. Yet once begun we cannot seem to leave it alone. How long before we're swallowing a horse?

This doesn't mean that the idea of improvement is somehow wrong. If a thing really does need improving and we possess the means to do so then why not give it a crack? We should, though, ensure that the means are not harmful (like the planned obsolescence that chokes our landfills with outdated gadgets), and its consequences do not leave one worse off than before (like the eviscerating "improvements" forced upon various cultures by a colonizing power). A harmless and helpful improvement is well worth the effort, and determining whether our interventions meet those criteria is part of the artistry of divine laziness. And so is deducing whether a thing needs improving at all. While it's true that a stitch in time saves nine, it's equally true that one should let sleeping dogs lie.

A mean and punishing regime

Do we even know how to leave things alone? Do we know how to stop? Even when there's nothing to do we glue to a screen or we shuffle through pages or something, anything to avoid the disorientation of just doing nothing. Just stopping, just sitting, perhaps a glance out the window or two. You'd think we'd be hungry enough to pounce on a chance to let the whole oppressive edifice crash to the ground for a glorious measure of sweet nothing. But on we are driven like people possessed, a demon in our minds screaming in protest at every cherished moment of peace we dare to snatch for ourselves. Is it any wonder we are bullied by stress and anxiety? It's a mean and punishing regime we're labouring under, made crueler by the fact that it is we ourselves who author its tenets.

We are not alone in this taxing campaign. Our allies come to the rescue—sugar, tobacco, caffeine—to prop us up when we flag, shake us to life and push us back into the fray. Many rely on this backup just to maintain the basic level of hyperactivity required of us. Enduring a day in the thick of it without these imbibements is unthinkable, and the fixes we schedule like stops on a journey allow us to ignore the annoying signs that we just need a rest. Our bodies and minds cry out for respite from the ceaseless travail, but their protests are drowned in yet another cup or hidden in the smog of another quickly rolled smoke.

As good as that is for the brewers and growers, the cost on a personal level is the wear and tear that comes from a lifetime of always being on, whether we're up to it or not. Meanwhile, the heart languishes; our innate longing for simple being, our idle wonder at the wild beauty of nothing special are stamped out by the boots of industry, yet again.

The consequences

A mind habituated to compulsive activity has little room for reflection upon the consequences of its actions. That's seen as drab and irrelevant: "Forget tomorrow, live for today; eat and drink, for tomorrow we may be dead" is the order of the day. All well and good for the forgetter, the eater, the drinker, but what about those whose lives our actions impact upon? Perhaps they don't fare so well in the wake of our frivolities.

How often does our negligence, our belligerence, our greed, throw up clouds that rain torment upon us and those around us? This is the real danger of a life lived aswirl in the maelstrom of compulsive doing: while we blunder around in a whirlwind of overactivity we can't even see, let alone safeguard, the things of our world that need a more delicate touch. Many of them just get blown to bits.

This is plainly evident on a personal level as we take stock of our overwrought lives. We see it also on larger scales in the volatility of warring countries tearing each other apart; in ecosystems punished and pushed to the brink of collapse; in a global community hopelessly addicted to consuming, choking on its own noxious outpourings. This long and sorry litany results from us doing what may have been left undone had we paused for reflection first.

Our bodies too bear the brunt of all this. In a thousand ways this excess is held as tension, rigidity, pain. Even at rest it is there, layer upon layer of it, hiding in shadows until the light of sensitivity flushes it out. But sensitivity is no welcome visitor, not in a body driven mercilessly on by a feverish need to get things done, and the signs and the symptoms of its torment go largely ignored. Until, that is, its protests get loud and urgent enough to bring the whole thing to a halt (hospital beds are a popular place to end up). Poor dear body, ridden like a warhorse up and down the front line, an unwitting victim in an ill-conceived war. Feel the fist of tightness as it clenches our guts. Feel the knots tying shoulders to neck. Feel how the jaw bites back its complaints. These are the traumas of a life in the firing line, abuses we pretend can be blamed on another. These are the signs that we've pushed it too far. This is the cost of spending more than we've got.

The roots

In light of all this we may wonder what drives this madness. What are the seeds that grow into such a tangle? There are many maps of the things that lie in the depths shaping human behaviour. For our purposes here a traditional Buddhist model serves us well (after all, the topography of divine laziness is coloured from a palette rich in Buddhist pigment). This viewpoint offers a simple and elegant outline of three roots that give rise to and nourish the entire organism of our dis-ease. These three drive us to manufacture all that can be considered unsettling, distressing or caustic in our experience. They go by the names of greed, aversion, delusion.

Greed is the full suite of hankerings that sees us always leaning out of this moment towards something else. Inherent in this leaning is an assumption that this moment just as it appears is not enough, and that some addition must be sought that will bring about a sense of completion, a state of happiness. The force of this yearning for what we don't have may range from the subtlest whisper of want to the deafening bellow of gale-force lust, but all of it involves our rejection of now in favour of some imagined better future. Or, we may have what we want and cling to it grimly lest fate or the slow decay of time takes it from us. This grasping has no let-up and gives no permission to slacken our grip. Greed is the stone in our shoe that fills our journey with torment and blisters. How can we relax, chafed by such grit?

Aversion is the inverse of greed: the cringing away from what we don't like. It is the displeasure we feel when confronted with something distasteful. It is the thousand little annoyances that can explode as anger and hatred. We seem to have an endless capacity for complaints about the way things are, and the grumbling and hostile mind has no more rest that the greedy one. Aversion turns our experiences sour, for it fixates on the solitary flaw amidst an infinitude of splendour. The push of aversion is what causes us to lash out in malice or cower in fear. It imagines harm in the innocent intentions of friends, and recasts them in our hearts as enemies and then again as demons. It sets us at war with the world and robs us of peace.

Delusion is the spectrum of misapprehensions that cloud our ability to see with clarity what's going on. This confusion is a background hum for most of us most of the time; we just don't see the full picture or understand the connotations of what we are doing. Hence, our activities are ill-advised. From simple misunderstandings or errors of judgment to the blind and numb oblivion of one who has lost all connection with the real, this inability to clearly perceive gives rise to the other two roots—greed and aversion—which spoil our actions and set us on an ill path.

Whatever form of agitation we experience, if we trace it back to its origin we will find at least one of these three roots feeding it.[2] They need not necessarily be dramatic or overt to work their mischief. Indeed, it is most often their subtle forms that have the most powerful effect over our behaviour, powerful precisely *because* they are subtle and hard to see, and therefore difficult to avoid.

For example, we don't need to be shoveling cakes into our face at a dinner party to be in the clutches of greed; even the slight leaning towards objects of our desire can be enough to colour our mood and intentions with the agitation of not having what we want. Likewise, our aversion need not be full-blown anger, hatred or disgust to bring abrasion to our experience; just the faint cringing away from experiences that we find distasteful sets us at odds with whatever is happening. And we need not be crushed in the grip of blunt confusion or blind ignorance to fall victim to the ingenious traps that delusion lays for us in each moment, for any moment that we don't see clearly or feel richly is a moment we may thus be ensnared.

Actions born of these roots are bound to push us around unkindly by virtue of their rotten ancestry. Once this is seen, steps may be taken to unyoke our behaviour from these tainted sources. This seeing and freeing is at the heart of divine laziness.

Without lifting a finger

A life insanely full and frantic leaves no room to stop and smell roses. No time have we to pause, relax, and enjoy the simple beauty of being alive. Unless, that is, we deliberately and purposefully move against the prevailing current of overactivity and sink back from the abrasive interface of doing into simple and purposeless being. Methods for cultivating this stepping-back have been part of our heritage as human beings all along, passed down through the meditative and contemplative traditions of all cultures. Some of these are drawn on in this book as it weaves from them a lifeline for those adrift and drowning in a sea of exertion.

This lifeline takes the form of a way of life—an art form, if you will—that we lovingly cultivate as, hand over hand, we draw ourselves free from the treacherous tide of overdoing and into an open territory of ease. This we can think of as the art of living effortlessly. One of the cardinal strands woven through this art form is the deeply mysterious Tao, whose wily sage Lao Tsu offers in his distinctive style—ever radical and absurdly rational—a pithy counter to the madness of overdoing:

> In the quest for knowledge, day by day something is gained.
> On the path of Tao, every day something is given up.
> Doing less and less, one finally reaches non-doing.
> Doing nothing, nothing is left undone.
>
> To govern the world, let it go its own way.
> We cannot control things by meddling.[3]

Such wisdom is sorely needed in a world rapidly digging itself into a hole. Further and faster does the light from the surface recede, and the walls of the shaft are about to collapse. Addicts of this digging we may be, but if we can manage to pull the anxious needle of overactivity out of our vein, perhaps we have a chance at doing less and less until non-doing is reached. Then, when nothing is left undone, we can take our interfering fingers out of so many pies and let things take their natural course, ruling the world without lifting a finger.

Wary of a tired ethos that would have us slaving day and night to feel a sense of worth, let us pen a new decree to live by: "Don't just do something; sit there!" Let us bend our backs not to task after pointless task, but in bowing down to kiss the ground where we have always stood. This is the art of divine laziness which fills the coming pages. This is the path of being no-one, going nowhere, doing nothing.

Chapter Two

Principles of Divine Laziness

AT ITS MOST REFINED level, divine laziness avoids any movement away from the present moment exactly as it is. It lets the universe be totally raw and unadorned as it rises and falls, completely at ease with it being just like this. It doesn't lift a finger. That kind of acceptance would totally free us from any need to meddle with this remarkable and utterly ordinary now. It would rest on a deep understanding that everything happening—exactly as it is happening—is entirely okay, and that any inclination to change things is just habitual movement of mind.

Few inhabit such a sublime state and perhaps few even wish to, but we needn't be so absolute. The art of living effortlessly can be cultivated at any level of refinement, from that pinnacle of profound non-doing to the relatively coarse level of just managing to curtail some of our more destructive behaviour.

In the Tao Te Ching—which has stood since its authoring in the sixth-century BC as one of the foundation stones of Chinese mystical and philosophical thought—it is written: "The Tao does nothing, yet nothing is left undone."[1] That Tao is the way of the universe, its modus operandi. It is the nature of existence itself, although as pointed out in the opening lines of the same book it really defies description: "The Tao that can be put into words is not the eternal Tao."[2]

The intervening millennia have, I'm sure, seen no shortage of ponderings upon these enigmatic statements. Who can say what their author really had in mind, but the concept of doing-nothing-yet-nothing-being-left-undone suggests an approach to life that is at once eminently effective and completely unforced, taking as its model the indefinable way of the universe itself. This approach doesn't try to resist the way it is, but accords with the natural flow of things. It takes the path of least resistance. It moves, when it moves, like water.

Be water, my friend

Water has much to teach us, if we care to learn, at least about how to flow. It always finds the way that offers the least resistance; it flows downhill, not up; it finds the lowest point and there it stays, still and clear, unmoved until circumstances compel it to change. Water shapes itself to any container without compromising its nature. Ultimately flexible, totally unbreakable. Even the mighty Bruce Lee looked to water as teacher and guide: "Empty your mind, be formless. Shapeless, like water. If you put water into a cup, it becomes the cup. You put water into a bottle and it becomes the bottle. You put it in a teapot, it becomes the teapot. Now, water can flow or it can crash. Be water, my friend."

Like water, events have their own flow. They have their own trajectory. It is best to let them go the way they are going and, if we need to interact, use their momentum to our advantage rather than trying to oppose. Harnessing the flow of water to generate electricity is a good example of this; we simply set up a mechanism to avail ourselves of the energy already and automatically being produced. To resist the water by stopping its flow would do us out of its power, so we let it do its thing: the water flows, the turbine spins, and we sit back and relax; a cup of tea perhaps, brought to the boil by virtue of the power being provided. Thus, nothing is done yet nothing is left undone.

Or, should we wish to claim a riverbed as dry and habitable land, we'd be fools to imagine we can stand against the river and command it to cease its advance. Rather, we employ the tactic of redirection, rerouting the river to our behest while never thwarting its flow. This strategy of redirection is well known to some; a skillful martial artist, for example, uses it to turn aside an attack while giving no ground nor wasting their energy by feeding the mouth of resistance. The same approach can be used to deal with whatever flows into our lives.

This is the way of according with the flow, going with the grain, letting the current carry us with it rather that fighting against it. This is the natural way to live, intelligent and efficient. Because this approach shies away from the use of force or effort where it's not needed, because it avoids doing when nothing needs to be done, we can call it laziness. And being in accordance with the workings of nature rather than moving or plotting against them—

feeling deeply the nuances of now—and because it results in harmony and avoids the misery of conflict, we can call it divine.

Not just sheer laziness

Laziness is a term that we have come to revile. Against a backdrop of pathological doing and the compulsive micromanagement of life's every aspect, our very sense of worth is defined by how much we do and achieve. It's no wonder the idea of laziness is frowned on as sinful. We would do well, then, to distinguish divine laziness from its derelict cousin sheer laziness. That run-of-the-mill, everyday laziness is merely the avoidance of doing what is needed, either because we lack sensitivity to the requirements of the moment and cannot feel what needs to be done, or we just no longer care. This kind of lethargy is not the art of living effortlessly.

Robbing us of the ability to touch our world and feel its pulse, depriving us of the senses that respond to life's prompts, sheer laziness holds us in the glue of inertia. It sends us lumbering into indolence. This is the road to ruin. In the art of living effortlessly it is wakefulness we nurture, not the barren sleep of heedlessness. An age ago the rewards of each were pointed out by the Buddha:

> Appreciative awareness leads to life;
> heedless avoidance is the path to death.
> Those who are aware are fully alive,
> while those who are heedless are as if already dead.[3]

We are done with the path of death. Let us set our hearts on being fully alive.

Divine laziness, then, is not the avoidance of effort per se, but learning to use our energy wisely and efficiently; what we do is done in a way that complements the flow of events and avoids the folly of fighting against them. We feel how things are moving and act in accordance with that, the way a sailor sets up his sails then lets the wind do the rest.

There is the recognition that in any given situation, much of what *could* be done *needn't* be, and this recognition gives rise to a natural inclination away from unnecessary effort. The sailor, of course, must remain sensitive to the changing requirements of the moment and adjust his sails accordingly. But for him to fill his lungs and blow into his sails in an attempt to go faster, or to try forcing his little boat against the mighty wind would be futile, exhausting, madness.

We bring this same attitude onto dry land to inform our behaviour in any endeavour. We recognize that we make life much, much harder for ourselves through needless tampering and habitual struggle. We make of the world a mighty adversary by assuming the role of antagonist and adopting a stance of resistance. This is a posture made painful by two crooked legs: not understanding the way things naturally flow, and the assumption that we can achieve what we want through brute force.

Going with it

It's true that much can be accomplished (or ruined, depending on your outlook) by hammering away at a thing like a caveman with a cudgel, but that kind of inelegance chases off optimum outcomes. Many would suggest that we humans have made great strides in "conquering" nature by bending the world to our will, and this is not untrue, but it should be remembered that whatever "progress" has been chalked up, there has also been made a considerable mess in the process. It should be remembered that truly liberating technologies work *with* the natural momentum of things, not against.

The recognition that each situation has its own natural momentum that can be ascertained and accorded with is a key. The door it unlocks is the ability to live in a way that is at once effortless (because any effort used is always the least required) and truly effective (because we act with the universe at our backs). Once we know where the energy of this moment is heading we go with it, adding a little something of our own if needed but otherwise just letting it go where it goes. Then, riding upon its momentum our effort becomes truly efficient.

This "going with" has about it a sense of harmony, the kind of harmony that is created when, for example, musicians play *with* the other members of the band and not against them, creating in the process something beautiful that is greater than the sum of its individual instrumental parts. Contentment and ease can flourish when we drop the drive to summon forth, through might or fight, a beautiful or excellent moment, and instead conspire with the beauty and excellence that is already here. We can relax and enjoy this remarkable now rather than missing it all while we fiddle and force.

The trick, of course, is that in order to go with whatever is happening we need to perceive clearly what's actually going on. We need to get a feel for now, to know its shape and how it moves, and that requires sensitivity. This sensitivity, as we shall see, is the agent that imbues our actions with effortlessness and renders our laziness useful and even—dare I say it—divine.

The effort of effortlessness

This does not mean that we simply let life tumble us along willy-nilly and never do anything to improve our situation. On the contrary, once we've tuned in to the shape and requirements of a situation we are able to respond with potent, even fierce efficacy. But we learn to sense whether improvement is needed at all or if things are doing just fine without us. If action or intervention is called for we step up and give it whatever we've got.

This may involve a great deal of effort—perhaps a veritable odyssey—but on the path of divine laziness any hardship is willingly undertaken when it's seen that the results are sure to be of benefit; to ourselves, to those around us, to the world at large. We roll up our sleeves and begin when we see that the effort involved in making a change for the better is but a drop when compared to the ocean of struggle that submerges us if those changes remain unmade. Those who fight for human rights or spread reform through a sickened land do so with great zeal and ardour. Their efforts, though taxing and prolonged, bring about a state of relative ease for many (and also for themselves as they reap the rewards of a benevolent heart), repaying a thousand times over any debt of energy spent in the process.

To stand by and do nothing while the mill of needless labour grinds on and on is a path far more costly in the long run. The man who's realized he's badly out of shape faces quite an ordeal when he undertakes a course of rehabilitation. His exertions are taken on not out of any love for labour but with the foresight that health and ease are mutually dependent. In the long run it's simply less effort—lazier, if you will—to work a little now so we may rest in the hammock of easeful conditions later.

The path of divine laziness takes us sometimes through a land beset with difficulty, but guides us always to a place of greater ease, a world made better by our endeavours. This is the effortless effort that, like water, inclines down the path of greatest ease. This is the doing that leads to non-doing, whose methods align with the way the cosmos unfolds. Acting thus, we stand upon the shoulders of a giant. Advancing thus, we sail before a mighty and benevolent wind indeed.

The course of action that attains the most while doing the least is the best one when something needs to be done. But maybe there is no problem here and things are already fine just as they are. Maybe nothing needs doing and all our efforts would only amount to fiddling. If so, we let it be. The heart of divine laziness, of living effortlessly, is the art of knowing when to move and when to stay still. Or maybe we'll discover even deeper what the Buddha meant when he spoke of a way that does neither:

> I crossed over the flood without pushing forward, without staying in place.
>
> When I pushed forward, I was whirled about. When I stayed in place, I sank.
>
> And so I crossed over the flood without pushing forward, without staying in place.[4]

As we navigate the deluge we dare not strain our limbs and break our hearts against the tide. Instead we find refuge in divine laziness, a sturdy ark that carries us safely through the torrent. Two principles make up the keel and the rudder of this simple vessel. They keep it afloat and they give it a shape. Those principles are effortlessness and sensitivity.

Effortlessness

Effortlessness means the avoidance of action that we know, through direct experience, will be useless or even harmful. Experiencing how tiresome it is to waste energy on futile ventures that lead to no good—like shouting at machines to get them to behave, like pelting the past with regrets or the future with worry —inclines us not to repeat them. We know it's not worth the effort. Likewise, if we can see that an impulse to act is growing in sordid soil we know it will yield a miserable crop so we don't pull it up to put on our plate. We just leave it where it is.

As we'll examine later in some detail, such foresight is gained through personal experience, and honed and developed through practice. Seeing how we invest our precious energy and get paid with a worthless or poisonous coin in return, we learn to reserve our effort to use only when it's required and where it will benefit. We lose interest in punishing ourselves with our own misplaced doings, just as we learn, through a thousand burned-out muscles, to act not in resistance but as a complement to the situation at hand.

This theme of non-resistance is central to many fields where skill is required, perhaps nowhere more visibly than in the martial arts, where dealing with force is a critical issue. Incoming force is not met with more force the way you would meet, say, a baseball by swinging a bat at it, but must be received and redirected if a battering is to be avoided.

In the context of a martial art, using this strategy makes it possible for a small person to overcome the onslaught of a bigger, stronger attacker by repurposing the assailant's superior physical force. They "borrow" their power. The defender avoids trying to out-muscle their burly opponent—which would surely be futile— and instead relies upon their own skill in reading and manipulating their opponent's energy to craft for themselves a successful defense.

This elegant strategy of non-resistance is the cornerstone of so-called "soft" martial arts, and enables practitioners to reach and maintain a remarkable, seemingly magical, level of skill well into advanced age. Morihei Ueshiba, the founder of the Japanese martial art Aikido (which is also called the Art of Peace) was teaching students right up until the time he died at the age of 85. This is how he praised non-resistance: "The Art of Peace is the principle of non-resistance. Because it is nonresistant, it is victorious from the beginning. Those with evil intentions or contentious thoughts are vanquished. The Art of Peace is invincible because it contends with nothing."[5]

Similarly, wing chun grandmaster Yip Man was still regularly training with (and outmaneuvering) his much younger students up until his last days, even when burdened by the cancer that ended his life at 79. Few exponents of "hard" or resistance-based martial arts can claim such longevity of practice, the rigours of force against flesh and bone cutting short too often their ability to embody their mastery. We'll examine non-resistance more closely in the context of wing chun kung fu later on (it's very close to my heart); for now we can simply note the efficiency of not wasting our efforts by straining against the powerful, but yielding instead and using that power to our own advantage.

This holding back from the fruitlessness of useless activity or the wasted struggle of resistance is the effortlessness that underpins divine laziness. We develop a sense of how tiresome it is to squander our efforts on profitless enterprise, so we just stop. We also get a distaste for the bitter consequences that shadow malicious or misguided behaviour. We see how those consequences pile themselves up as a cumbersome load that asks to be carried around, and we grow too lazy to shoulder that burden. We leave it where it is. This is the right kind of laziness.

Right effort

Occupying a prominent place in classical Buddhist thought (which has informed much of my own exploration into effortlessness) is the concept of right effort. This fourfold categorization deals with our mental efforts, the work we put our minds to. It outlines how those efforts should be steered if they are to be effective and worthwhile. According to this framework, the four ways we can use effort well are:

- Avoiding unskillful states that have not yet arisen

- Abandoning unskillful states that have arisen

- Encouraging skillful states that have not yet arisen

- Maintaining skillful states that have arisen

Right effort turns away from unskillful states and towards those that are skillful. Mindstates described as unskillful are those infused with greed, hatred or ignorance, like selfishness, belligerence and malice. Tools of discord, they beat us black and blue. Wary of such a pummeling, right effort gives them a wide berth. Should they have arisen, though, we drop them where we stand. Skillful states, on the other hand, tend towards well-being, freedom and ease. These are states devoid of harm, steering clear of discord and rising and falling in harmony.

Our task, should we wish to walk the way of divine laziness, is to attune ourselves to these states within us. Then, as their presence or absence is known, we take them up or let them go accordingly. Just as defining as the mind states we inhabit are those that we avoid. Just as important as what we do is what we do not.

Through experience and experimentation we come to know the likely outcome of present actions of body and mind. Those that we know will bring happiness and ease we care for and cultivate and make them a home. But those that are likely to cause us distress, sowing discord within or without, we abandon or put to one side, dropped like burning coals. Effort is made to ensure they are kept at bay in the future or avoided entirely; wary of their danger, we sidestep them or turn away when they darken our course of action. This is the knack of non-doing, the key to useful laziness.

Activities outside the fourfold field of right effort will not treat us kindly. At best they exhausts us, wasting our energy. More likely, though, we craft for ourselves a path fraught with misery that leads through a land of distress. A path like this is not of our choosing but is nevertheless of our doing, for anything we do is the cause of effects which in turn are the causes of yet more effects. We build the future deed by present deed.

This is not to say, though, that we should become paralyzed with fear of doing the wrong thing and then being burdened by its unwanted consequences. Although such inertia may appear to be playing it safe, it stops us from living and slays spontaneity before it is born. For it is not spontaneity itself but unskillful, habitual reflexes that lead to a future disfigured by the unappealing results of our own foolishness.

We avoid such a drab mode of operating by aiming our effort in the right direction, in a way that will have a useful or desirable outcome and will not leave us worse off than not having acted at all. This involves becoming sensitive to the requirements of each moment and acting accordingly. In feeling the tone of each moment we also feel how we need to respond. That feeling faculty is the other principle of divine laziness: sensitivity.

Sensitivity

The extent to which effortlessness is available to us depends on the level of sensitivity present: sensitivity to the shape and contents of a situation and the way its energy flows. When this sensitivity is present we are able to respond in a harmonious way. The greater the harmony, the less energy we squander in resistance.

Sensitivity is the mark of divine laziness, differentiating it from sheer laziness. It allows us to determine what response (if any) is appropriate to the situation at hand, and to act (or not) accordingly, distinguishing those who act in true accord with the moment from those who just do out of habit. Through deliberate sensing and choosing of how to behave we spontaneously engage with the present moment in a way that is intimate and alive. We feel for and deploy the most congruous course of action, the course that is richest in effortlessness.

Sometimes I go walking barefoot in the woods or on a trail. (If you haven't done that, you should.) During one such excursion it hit me how insulated we are from the terrain we traverse when we wrap our feet up in footwear. Shielding us from the character and texture of the ground underfoot, shoes hoodwink us out of relationship with that environment. But slip off your shoes and walk a while and a whole universe of feeling is born in the space between soil and sole.

Making contact with the ground on which we stand, we feel the where and touch the here of it. The surface beneath us dictates how we move, and our soles and our bodies respond with intuitive virtuosity. Step on a stone and we instantly do the dance that softens around it and seeks beyond it. Concrete and moss and pebbles and mud each have something to say about how we behave as we walk on them, and instinctively we respond. Swaddle our feet, though, in inches of rubber and banish that world from experience; we can get away with blatant indifference to terrain that would otherwise demand great skill and delicacy to navigate. Try it: we can walk with our feet flaccid and dead when they're trussed up in shoes; those wonderful instruments, perfectly designed for informing our movements, slapping along like a couple of boneless fillets. Feeling nothing, we care nothing as we ride roughshod over the lot of it.

Unearthing our sensitivity is much like this, waking up to the ways that we flop through our lives encased in a full-being shoe. Thick and well-heeled, this casing allows us to crash along with nary a glimpse of the flowers we crush or the stones we don't feel through its thick and soulless sole. Heedless of posture and cadence and gait we recklessly charge on ahead. But we who would shake sensitivity from its slumber are tasked with divesting ourselves of that shoe, with exposing ourselves to the harsh or delicious experience of being right here. And the instrument of feeling, thus exposed, might surprise us with its expertise at feeling the shape of now and directing the perfect response.

We all have some degree of innate sensitivity; to social cues, to our own needs or the needs of others, to environmental factors that impact on how we should or even can behave. We take this in with our mother's milk and add to it as we move through life's various training grounds. But developing our sensitivity beyond that baseline can free us from a curriculum of merely acting and reacting according to our conditioning. It grows our ability to feel and respond to the needs of the moment.

As we begin to feel more we may notice how often we blunder around, blind to the effects of our actions. And as sensitivity grows we begin to perceive what is actually going on, both internally (within our own minds and bodies) and externally (pertaining to the environment we're in). Awareness dawns of the likely results of our conduct, and that awareness informs how we behave.

With this sharper vision we also see that our present state is largely created by what we have done in the past. Things cause other things to happen, and those other things are flavoured by the things that caused them. The cause stamps its likeness upon the effect. An understanding of cause and effect is the linchpin of any genuine system of moral or ethical training. It holds together the art of living effortlessly.

Cause and effect

The cause-and-effect process is often referred to as "karma." This word has found its way into common parlance as a label for the mechanism of cause and effect in general (usually with the addition of a mystical or magical component, and connotations of it being some punitive agent of divine retribution meting out justice to those who've done wrong). Perhaps we are guilty of using this idea as justification for our own mistreatment of others (he deserved it; it was his karma to be treated like that), or as an excuse for turning away from those in need (there's nothing I can do; they've got to work out their own karma). Or perhaps we pin our hopes on some kind of "good karma" we feel we've earned due to the many great things we've done. Karma, however, is neither good nor bad, neither saviour nor persecutor, and such pop-definitions hopelessly deform the idea and miss the point by a mile.

Karma is a Sanskrit word[6] denoting a mechanism that plays a pivotal role in the philosophical and ethical frameworks of Indian thought (particularly Buddhism and Hinduism). It simply and literally means "action." However, implicit in the term karma is the idea that any action has consequences or results. The actual results of action are referred to in these systems by a different word: vipaka, which means the results of intentional action, the ripening or maturation of karma. So, the whole cause-and-effect process is defined as karma-vipaka—action and its result.

The thrust of traditional teachings on karma is that every action has inevitable and inescapable results which either bring us happiness and freedom or bind us more tightly to thorns of misfortune and misery. Those results may be very subtle, such as the vague uneasiness felt when we fill our thoughts with hatred, or crashingly obvious, like the battering we get when we drive our car into a tree. But big or small, for better or worse, the effect is set in motion by the act and cannot be wished away. Traditional teachings leave no room for doubt about this:

> There is no place on earth
> where one can hide
> from the consequences of evil actions –
> not in a mountain cave,
> the ocean nor in the sky.[7]

And, for those of a more poetic bent, the words of Omar Khayyam in their most beautiful and lucid arrangement:

> The Moving Finger writes; and, having writ,
> Moves on: nor all thy Piety nor Wit
> Shall lure it back to cancel half a Line,
> Nor all thy Tears wash out a Word of it.[8]

Nor do the inevitable sequels to those indelibly written chapters necessarily appear on the very next page; they may take a long while to show up. But show up they will, of that we can be certain.

We tend to stand up as accountable for only those results that follow an action immediately; any time lag between the two give us occasion to ready the finger of blame. But results of actions often show up long after the event. By this time we may well have forgotten all about the original act, and probably see no correlation between it and our current plight. We blame it all on chance, and fail to see the weeds that choke our lives have sprung from seeds we planted long ago. We have not got off scot free; we just cannot feel the chains that bind us.

Even when a time lag does appear to separate action from result, the planting from the ripening, their correlation can be as directly observable as the "instant karma" of touch-fire-burn-hand. A commonplace example like planting an apple tree makes this clear: much time elapses before we get to eat apples, but the cause and effect relationship between putting the seed in the ground and the first crunch of fruit is undeniable.

This time lag between cause and effect is one further reason why mainstream culture so misunderstands the concept of karma. It has been mythologised as the vague sentiment "what goes around comes around," the murky sense that if I step on a spider in this life then in some imagined future I'll end up as a spider being crushed beneath a shoe. Or that if I lash out in violence then some future person will beat me black and blue. This cartoon view, although entertaining and containing a kernel of truth, is not much use from a pragmatic point of view as it does little to encourage us to scrutinize and take responsibility for our actions (other than perhaps introducing an ill-defined sense of fear and guilt into our doings).

Actions are like stones thrown into a pool; they make a splash or send out ripples according to their gravity. Even if they roll in softly and sink to the bottom unnoticed, still they change the topography of the pool and alter the shape of all the water it contains. While we are unable to feel within ourselves the results of what we do, there is little motivation for us to act with care. But as our sensitivity develops we realize more and more that everything we do makes waves—some of them pleasant to ride, some of them tsunamis of great destructive power—and we feel those waves within us, and we see them wash over those around us. Divested of the mantle of dullness, we no longer can fool ourselves that we may do as we please, for each deed is felt as a slap or caress the moment we turn it loose on the world.

Although any action inevitably plants the seeds of consequence, we must remember it's the intention behind those actions that determine the shape of its results, not the action itself. Actions may be deliberate or completely accidental. We can't control everything we do: sometimes our clumsiness results in broken crockery; sometimes we drive into a bird as it flies across the road. But we can examine our intentions as they start to push us out onto the stage. We can choose whether or not to read the lines and do the dance which has us taking a bow to the roar of applause or slinking from the scene in disgrace. Consider the following two acts:

1. A surgeon cuts into a patient's abdomen to perform an operation

2. A murderer stabs his victim in the belly

The physical actions are clearly the same (that of piercing someone's body with a blade), but the intentions behind them are a universe apart. In the case of the surgeon the intention is a compassionate one—alleviating the patient's discomfort—and the effect on both the surgeon and the patient is likely to be positive. In the case of the murderer however, the intention is undoubtedly cruel and the effect on both parties will not incline towards happiness.

Our intentional actions create results that we ourselves are the recipients of, and the intention behind those actions determines the nature of those results. Karma therefore knows nothing of some external agency that punishes us for screwing up or bestows upon us treats when we're good. It's a simple and observable fact that we verify for ourselves, a natural law that operates perpetually whether we know it or not, and seeks not our consent in the matter.

Seeing as there is no escaping the results of our own actions we'd do well to stick to doing things that are likely to bring results we actually want. Through experience and wise reflection we start to get a feel for the kinds of results we can expect from the various species of action available to us. This is the sensitivity that enables us to dexterously navigate the landscape of doing; to cultivate skillful action that brings about harmony and to avoid sowing seeds of disaster.

As we move through life now sensitive and alive, not only do we feel our way through the process of acting and reaping results, we also sense the weight of the burden we carry by constantly overdoing. Noticing how we drag that burden around, exhausted, we finally see that we can just stop and give up. The idea of quitting is no longer seen as a weakness, a failing, a sin. Instead we rejoice in the freedom that comes when we step off the treadmill that keeps us running only to stay where we are.

This is the radical act of one driven sane by sensitivity. What we stop is the constant doing of that which needn't be done. What we give up is the dis-ease of trying to crush the universe into a shape that it's not. What we quit is the project of futile resistance. Far from a weakness, this is the strength to wake up in a world that is screaming its way through a nightmare. In place of brute force and fruitless activity comes an effortless engagement with life, flowing with and not pushing against, resting in the ease of laziness and humming with the harmony of the divine.

And so we find in these two principles—sensitivity and effortlessness—the foundations of divine laziness. Principles alone, however, will not make one adept. For that a third component is needed. That third component is training, which gives us a means to fashion those principles into a living reality. The next chapter explores how these three elements bring one another to life.

Chapter Three

Developing Divine Laziness

HAVING EXAMINED THE PRINCIPLES of sensitivity and effortlessness upon which divine laziness finds its footing, we can look at how the process of training breathes life into those principles, and how that breath is returned. Taken together, these three elements—training, sensitivity and effortlessness—form an interdependent cycle of development. This cycle is the process by which divine laziness is cultivated, what I have come to think of as the enlazening process.

In the development of our art of living effortlessly—or any art form we may feel called to pursue—it is by this threefold process that we gradually attune ourselves to the postures and instruments of that art form and refine our actions to accord with its nuances. This process brings an art to life within us and instills it in our hearts as the beating engine of our engagement with life. It's a simple engine, but powerful, and as it carries us through stages of artistry our task is to keep it in tune. But first let's see what's under the hood.

Remember playing paper/scissors/rock? Each played hand defeats one of the other two and is defeated in turn by the third: scissors cut paper, paper wraps rock and rock blunts scissors. The threefold process of development can be visualised as something rather like that, with its three operants—training, sensitivity and effortlessness—acting upon one another in a similar fashion (though as benefactors rather than subduers), like so:

- Training develops our sensitivity

- Sensitivity enables effortlessness

- Effortlessness brings finesse to our training, rendering it more efficient and effective

- More effective training develops further still our sensitivity, which allows for greater effortlessness, which facilitates more effective training, further enhancing sensitivity, and so on

The interplay between these three elements thereby creates a feedback loop where the output is returned as input back into the interplay. Each element augments the next while being augmented by the third: training develops sensitivity, sensitivity develops effortlessness, effortlessness develops training.

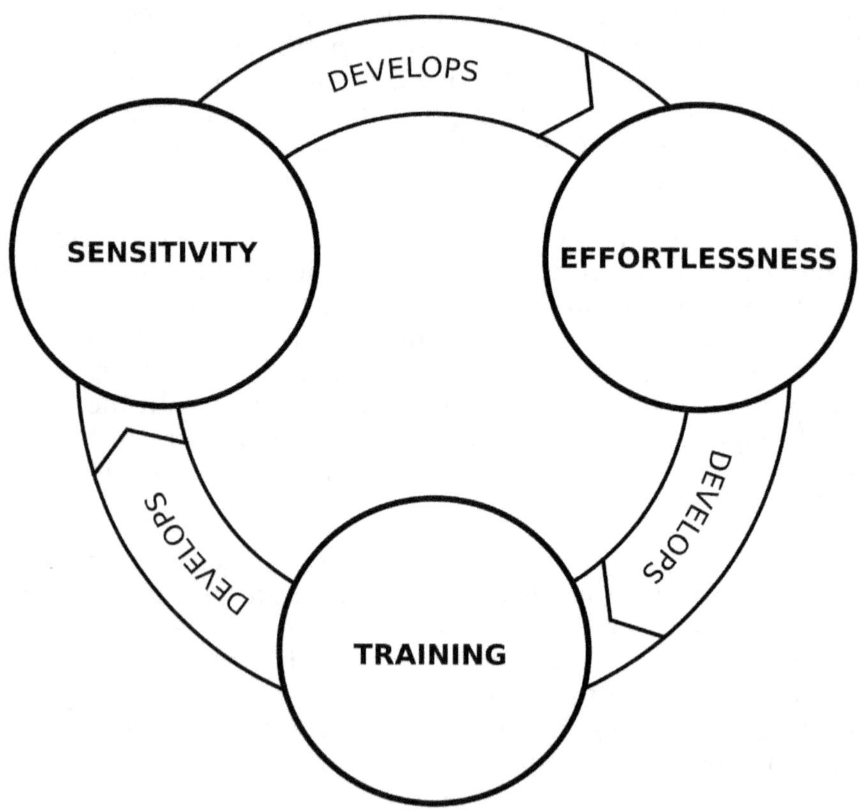

FIGURE 1: The threefold process of development

Training develops sensitivity

Training calls us to repeatedly do a thing until it has been perfected. But mere repetition won't make of us masters, and training is made of several parts: learning the principles upon which the art or skill is based; adhering to rules that guide our actions in certain directions; persistent doing of it over and over again. And always that training seeks to draw us beyond what we're currently capable of.

As we take ourselves time and again to the edge of our competence and beyond, not only do we feel more keenly the poor form and clumsiness that blemish our actions, but we register how far those actions fall short of ideal. It is the common experience of any who take up an art form that the more we progress, the further we feel we are from where we are aimed. This is not due to a lessening of skill, but rather to a quickening of the faculties that gauge the length of the journey to mastery. There grows our sensitivity.

That sensitivity feels how an action ought to be done, and how far that is from what we are actually doing. It sees well the ground to be covered between, and knows well the tasks that make up that course. Chief among these is the task of divesting ourselves of the heavy-handed effort that spoils the attempts of the novice.

Sensitivity develops effortlessness

As we trust in that sensitivity and pay heed to its guidance we fathom more clearly the role of effort in action. We notice how and where our energy leaks away, squandered on doing that which does not need to be done, or on overdoing that which does. We see how heavy-handedness spoils our efforts, like tuning a radio with a sledgehammer, like weeding a flowerbed with a bulldozer, like plucking a guitar string with all of our might.

As our familiarity with the tools and techniques of an art form grows—whether they be the instruments of music, the bodily movements of dance or kungfu, or the well-placed no-doings of effortless living—we tune the amount and quality of effort we use to fit the requirements of whatever is happening. Then, when we act, we do just enough to achieve what is needed without wasting energy on the extraneous. We do the least to accomplish the most.

Effortlessness develops training

Freed from unnecessary effort our training becomes efficient and effective. Once we see it takes more than a hammer to build something, we are able to choose the right tools for the task at hand, and to use them well. We only do what is required, in a way that is appropriate, and as our artistry grows and deepens so too does our understanding of what is meant by required, and what the shape of appropriate is. The effort we use in our training is measured by quality rather than quantity. A little bit at the right time in the right place is gold.

This cycle of mutual enhancement is also a cycle of mutual dependence: the ability to embody effortlessness depends upon sensitivity; sensitivity depends upon training; and training, if it is to be fruitful, depends upon our approaching it with increasing effortlessness. So, without training we cannot hope to develop sensitivity. And as we have seen in the foregoing chapters, sensitivity is the enabler of effortlessness. While we have not a measure of effortlessness to bring finesse to our training, that training amounts to little more than boorish repetition. Artistic development depends upon all three of these elements being in tune.

The cyclic nature of this process brings to mind the image of a helix or a coiled spring; each "revolution" of the cycle (training developing sensitivity, sensitivity developing effortlessness, effortlessness developing training) puts us, in a sense, back where we started (in this case, back in the territory of training). But we have also advanced *forward* along a third dimension. That is, our training is now more effective than before by virtue of the sensitivity and effortlessness it has given rise to, and with which it is now infused. We have progressed. At each conceptual spin around the coil we find that all three factors of training, sensitivity, and effortlessness have been refined and enhanced through the influence of the others. We're not just going around and around, we are moving onward and upward as well.

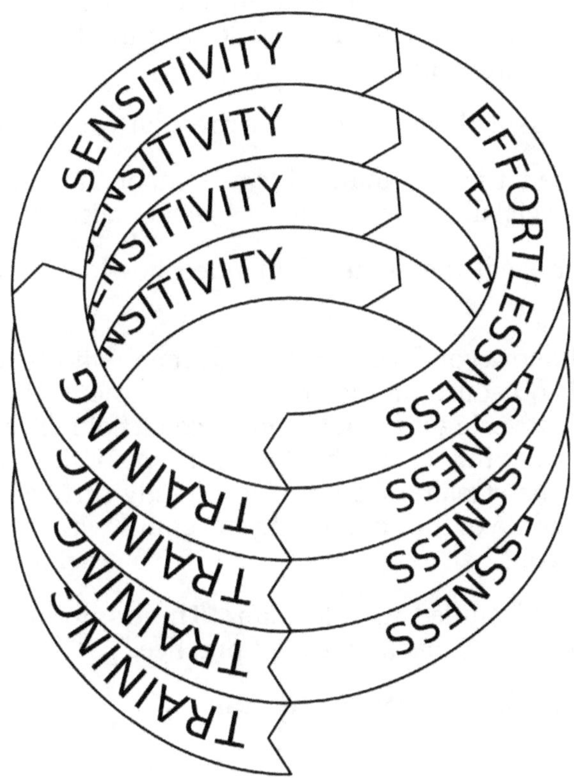

FIGURE 2: The spiral of mutual enhancement

Just a matter of practice

Fancy as all this may sound, it's only the ordinary process an artist goes through when learning their art. And climbing that process to great skill is nothing outrageous, it's just a matter of practice.

There is an old Chinese parable about a great archer who learned that his talents were nothing special. The archer was demonstrating his considerable skill one day, surrounded by an admiring audience. Arrow after arrow he fed to the bullseye, and drank the applause from all those around. All? No, there was one; an old oil-seller. Not so impressed, this old man simply nodded his head as each shot found its mark. Seeing this, the archer, incensed, confronted him:

"Are you so skilled with bow and arrow that you can do better?"

"No," replied the old man, "I can't shoot at all. But there's nothing so special about your skill. It's just a matter of practice."

Further enraged, the archer demanded how dare the old timer speak to him so.

"Look, I'll show you," replied the old man, who then set about arranging his oil gourd on the ground before them. Upon the neck of the gourd, covering its mouth, he placed a coin. Then, standing up with a ladle full of oil he began to pour. To the archer's amazement, the stream of oil passed directly through the square hole in the middle of the coin, filling the gourd without a drop ever touching the coin.

"No big deal," smiled the old man. "There's nothing so special about this either. It's just a matter of practice."

Humbled, the archer went on his way.

I first heard this story from my sifu[1] shortly after I began my study of wing chun kung fu. (It's worth a quick look at this art form here because wing chun offers a vivid example of the threefold enlazening process at work. It's got sensitivity and effortlessness written all over it, and they become harder to ignore the further training progresses.) He told me this story to drive home a point that would be made time and again over the coming years: if we want to get good at something we have to practice. And if we practice often and well we can't help but develop great skill.

He added to the tale of the archer and oil-seller a Chinese maxim, roughly translated as "When techniques are practiced many times, the art becomes familiar." Through repetitive practice of a thing it becomes well known, integrated, assimilated. It becomes natural.

Wing chun, though, feels anything but natural at first. At least it was that way for me. Techniques of hand and posture and stance felt remarkably awkward back at the start. Nevertheless, through struggle and strain they gradually came to feel more like things that a body could actually do. Things that could be done precisely yet naturally. Things that could even be done while relaxed. And only once those moves came to be second nature could they be used as the instruments of sensitivity that wing chun is built around.

That sensitivity is the key to using the techniques and tactics that we have so painstakingly nurtured. It tells us when to move and how, and it teaches us how to stay still. Without sensitivity, what we are left with in a practice like wing chun is not far removed from the playground wrestling of schoolboys.

As this sensitivity develops we also learn about how to use energy: too much and we hand our partner the tools with which to defeat us; too little and our structure collapses in ruins. At this stage it is the skillful use of effortlessness—what I have come to think of as the right kind of laziness—that we must gradually cultivate. As that laziness takes hold, new aspects of old and familiar techniques are revealed, and our training becomes more refined. Which leads to more sensitivity. Which leads to more effortlessness. And so it goes on. And so our skill grows, even for someone as artless to start with as me.

Other examples

Let's take another example, one that most of us know: the process of learning a language. At first we gather the few basic words required to just get us by. We stumble through phrase after fairly embarrassing phrase, taking a rough stab at pronunciation. We try to make sense of grammatical rules and the labyrinth that is semantics, but we lack sensitivity to the nuances required to make anything more of our speech than the rudimentary.

Through practice, however, we start to get more of a taste for how the words should sound and feel as we form them. We learn, quite formally and rigidly, the rules of grammar and semantics upon which we begin to build conversation. Effort and vigilance are our constant companions at this stage, with frequent reference to those rules to make sure what we're talking is sense and not gibberish.

It's hard work, but as practice continues and sensitivity grows we no longer clutch the rulebook so tightly. We start to hear more and can say more. We feel more keenly the subtle cues that inhabit our conversations, cues that inform the tone we should use, the words we should choose, the aptness of comedy or gravity. Less effort is used, both in speaking and in reaching for the right words. We become more adept. This makes our practice that much more fruitful; we have more tools, and more refined tools, to use in our practice. Then, as we begin to master the language we cast off the rulebook entirely. Conversation flows and we respond according to what we intuitively know is appropriate. We seldom need to stop and think of which words we should use; the right ones just happen, effortlessly.

Or, say we want to become a musician. Having acquainted ourselves with the principles governing music, we take on the training that builds the techniques needed to play our chosen instrument. As our techniques improve so too does our sensitivity. We develop a feel for the instrument and the music being played, and we learn to control the energy we use and direct it according to what is required. The more we practice, the more that sensitivity grows. The more sensitive we are, the more finely tuned and effortless our playing becomes, and so are revealed more subtle realms of practice and development, their once hidden riches becoming available to us.

A friend of mine is a classical guitarist who's been practicing for many years. He explained to me one day how the subtlest change in technique can have a noticeable effect on the sound and feel of the music being played. There is a guitar technique called a slur, where the finger of the fretting hand hammers on to the string to make a jump from one note to the next. The finger that hovers but a millimeter from the string, rather than an inch away, requires a smaller amount of effort to execute the slur. That ease can be heard in the feel of the music, the difference between sound that is forced and aggressive, and that which is smooth and relaxed.

Such a small detail, but small details are the veils that separate novice from master. The ability to deliver that effortless slur only comes about through endless hours of fine-tuning, and the sensitivity of fingers and ears that such training develops. Without that training, that sensitivity, that effortlessness, we only make clumsy and discordant attempts at guitar play.

The art of living effortlessly is just as concerned with fine-tuning and just as wary of clamour. Its training ground is every now and it asks us to bring that finesse into every here. Setting our hearts on this path, everything we do becomes our magnum opus, and through whole-hearted refinement we make it a monument worthy of spending a life on.

Whatever the art form being pursued, its cultivation is just this threefold process: training enhanced by effortlessness; effortlessness enhanced by sensitivity; sensitivity enhanced by training. And if that art form be based upon natural principles— those found to be operant in the workings of the universe itself— its mastery engenders a laziness that is truly divine.

Awa Kenzo, a true master of kyudo, the Japanese art of archery, spent much of his life steering his students along the way that leads to great freedom and ease. The clue he left for determining an art form's capacity to lead us that far was this: "True art makes you want to bow your head in reverence."[2]

This reverence, then, is the touchstone that tells us our art is the study of how the universe moves. For when, through our art, we draw near to the heart of all, we cannot help bowing our heads. And as we feel the steering hand of nature at work as we act, we defer to its apt and infallible guidance. We practice our art to follow the way that moves in accordance with natural law, and that is art for heart's sake. So let us make of our lives such an art form. Let us craft from our days and our nights, by way of this threefold enlazening process, a simple and beautiful masterpiece.

Chapter Four

Rules and Freedom

THE FIRST MONK I met, many years ago, made a comment that has stayed with me since. He was often asked why his vocation demands obedience to so many rules if it's supposed to be about freedom. As a Buddhist monk he was living by 227 precepts that govern many minute details of daily life; how can that be freedom? His response to this question was another: "Do we have the freedom to live within those rules?"

What a question! It sat me down and made me consider the average take on freedom. Many of us when faced with the prospect of living under such a regime would most likely run to the hills. The idea of going without our indulgences or restraining our behaviour is most unwelcome. We are, in effect, bound like slaves to a fantasy of being able to do whatever we want. This is clearly not freedom. So the idea that one could develop the freedom to live according to consciously chosen guidelines, however stifling they may seem from the outside, for the purpose of cultivating a life of happiness and ease was a breath of fresh air. A breath like that can fill our sails on a journey into ever-deepening freedom.

At a glance it may seem the two notions of rules and freedom are mutually exclusive: one can either live by rules, which is not living freely, or one can live freely, which is not living by rules. But that is a flimsy grasp of both the concept of rules and the meaning of freedom. It imagines freedom as doing whatever we please, with no-one telling us how to behave. This, of course, is no approximation of reality; we seldom if ever get to do what we want, no matter how firmly we assert that we are in control. (Not to mention how only ever doing as we please deprives us of all the options that doing as we *don't* please would give us).

We assume our behaviour is freely chosen by us. But so many of our actions are automatic, programmed responses to whatever is happening. So much of what we do is conditioned by whatever societal context we find ourselves in and governed by the rules it has etched in our hearts. Even our modes of thinking—the perceptions and attitudes that seem to make up the very fabric of who we are—amount to little more than mental habits built by the cultures we've grown in. True, we do have some power to make choices; we can choose to act on our impulses or not, even if we cannot prevent or control their arising. It is this ability to choose that makes training ourselves a possibility. But unless we embark upon such a course of training, deliberately sculpting our behaviour to accord with a chosen ideal, it will be the same old automatic societal conditioning that holds sway over how we conduct ourselves. That training marks out a path from the land of automata onwards and upwards to freedom.

Inner rules

Freedom from what, we may ask? How about freedom from enslavement to the unconscious "rules" that are wrought as we grow; rules we obey without question, without even knowing we're doing so. These are the prescripts that surreptitiously impose their injunctions: "No-one can tell me what to do; I have a right to this; It's me or them; Never admit defeat; Never show your weaknesses; Keep it together." And so on, and on and on and on.

Whatever may be our own species of inner laws, be sure that while they are unseen and unknown they have us in their jaws. Unconscious, unspoken, they occupy the throne. We scurry to obey with never a query as to what authority has sanctioned their edicts. We hold up these statutes as shining examples of our freedom and individuality, yet down we bow to them and do their bidding, while derision for the squares who follow the rules falls out of our mouths.

To bring these rules into the light of awareness robs them of most of their power, for they cannot steal our autonomy from under our noses while our eyes are on them. When we see them as no more than the pages of our own internal rulebook we can decide whether or not they carry the weight and substance that deserves our obedience. Perhaps in the clear light of day a great many will be seen to fall short of that measure; these we are best to scratch from our blueprint of living.

Perhaps some we may keep and befriend anew as we see them to be built on virtue: "Always brush your teeth after eating; Men should never hit women (or men, for that matter. Or children. Or dogs, or cows, or television sets...); Listen twice as much as you speak (two ears, one mouth)." Et cetera. Gems such as these, once recognised for what they are—inner rules that guide our behaviour unnoticed—and chosen instead as components of a conscious creed, speak to us now with a different voice. No longer the subterranean nagging that makes of us goody-goods and robs us of genuine virtue, their voice in our ear becomes trusted and clear, like timely advice from a friend.

One way we can unearth these rules and shine the light of seeing upon them is to impose, quite intentionally, a different set of rules of our own choosing; rules weighed up as to their merit and reasonableness; rules complied with willingly and purposefully. Then, once we've accepted their boundaries, trusting that their positive results will more than offset any perceived inconvenience, we may notice when allegiances to old unconscious rules are at odds with the requirements of the new ones. This gives us the cause and the opportunity to see and examine the old and, if need be, to begin discarding them. As we observe that rules designed to flavour our actions with skillfulness, when embraced consciously and deliberately, pay back our allegiance with freedom and ease, we gladly abandon habitual creeds to the contrary that would trap us in their miserable results.

The learning of an art form furnishes us with a vivid example of this. Its training regime works to override or replace embedded unconscious rules with consciously chosen alternatives. When we embark upon learning an art form we carry with us the burden of habits that dictate how we move, how we act and behave. Much of this needs to be shorn away and replaced with new modes of moving, of acting, of behaving specific to our art form if we are to progress in its cultivation. And submission to its clearly defined and rigorous scaffold of training—with its rules that demand we jettison habitual ways of behaving and painstakingly cultivate new ones—is just the ticket.

Training: principles

Deep beneath the surface of our world lie ancient bones. They are the laws of nature, the skeletal principles that shape its flesh and allow it to move in certain ways. Art forms are also built around principles, and these define how the artist should work in bringing their art to life. If we want to enter an art form and climb up its scaffold of training then first we must take a firm grasp of its principles. How closely we know them, how well we align with them governs how free our expression of that art will be.

And if that art form is one that is true (one that makes you want to bow your head) it rests on the bones of nature and is therefore the study of how the universe moves. Mathematics, for example, is based upon principles of nature, observed and systematized by people observant enough to do so. By learning and aligning with these principles the mathematician is able to operate with great freedom within the sphere of mathematics, doing things with numbers that are beyond comprehension to a mathematical dunce (like me). One with such skill appears to enjoy the view into workings of nature through a window that remains opaque to the rest of us.

Music as well is inherent in nature, discovered by humans (and birds), studied and systematized gradually (by the humans more than the birds, I suppose). The relationship of various notes to each other, like octaves or fifths or diminished thirds, is the same no matter who plays it, no matter what the instrument or where in the world it is played. Timing is similarly constant, and tempo and rhythm as well. Combinations of tones that we call minor chords evoke a response that we label melancholic; those we call major evoke what we think of as cheerful. The musician who understands how these principles interact with each other, and with the human beings lending their ears, can manipulate tones and tempo to convey a feeling; they can bring us to rapture or tears.

Whether mathematics or music, whether painting, kung fu or the art of living effortlessly, an art form is ruled by its principles. They provide a container and a context for its expression, a framework for transforming action into beauty, and those who have trained well can make this transmutation effortlessly. Perhaps only dimly acknowledged at first, the principles of an art form become ever more deeply beheld as training progresses. That understanding, if taken to heart, allows us to move about freely within the scope of that art form, using the skills and artistry our training has furnished us with.

So it is with the bones of divine laziness, the sensitivity and effortlessness that lie in its depths: they are the signposts that show us where the road lies, the curbs that direct us as we make our way into the heart of it, and the ridgepole and rafters around which we build a sturdy edifice of effortless living.

Training: rules

Aside from its principles, an art form also needs a system of man-made rules that govern our actions if training is to bear fruit. Rules regulate what we may do in our training and what we may not. Within their restraining embrace our actions are greatly simplified, the range of options available to us limited to only the useful. Although they constrain us—*because* they constrain us— these rules are the keys that turn in the locks of our art form, and give us the freedom to act with effectiveness. Misguided and useless activity is put aside as we focus on only those actions that nurture our aims.

The skill of our mathematician, for example, must be developed by following rules set up for the purpose of developing those skills. Training exercises are learned and applied, practiced again and again, and dexterity grows. Without this period of training (except I imagine in cases of genius) the mathematician would likely be a very poor one; few of us wake up one morning to discover we are able to perform advanced calculus out of the blue. The same goes for the musician, the painter, the dancer; all have built their prowess upon a foundation of well-guided training.

So too with our journey into divine laziness. Having recognised the principles paving the pathway of effortless living, we also have seen that to move on that path requires the vehicle of training. Our conduct is sublimated and our actions are tempered in the crucible of a code of discipline, and that code is built upon rules. They paint a red line, those rules, around actions that summon disaster. They gather our wayward mindstates and point them as one at the heart of ease. And we abide by them willingly once we see they are leading us to freedom. (The shape and substance of such a rule-set is covered in following chapters.)

Training without rules to guide us is no training at all; to flitter about on the wings of our whims, now here, now there, will fail to get us anywhere. We can understand the principles of an art form all we like, but without some actual training governed by expedient guidelines we never get within shouting distance of artistry.

The (seeming) paradox of rules and freedom

It seems paradoxical that the effort to practice within a constraining set of rules is the very thing that enables us to act with effortlessness and freedom (once a certain degree of proficiency has been reached). But it is just this adherence to well-defined training rules, and diligent application of effort to training, that brings about freedom and effortlessness.

Without rules there can be no training; without training, and the sensitivity and effortlessness it engenders, skill does not develop; without skill in our art form, though we pound on them with all of our ill-suited might, the doors to freedom of artistry remain firmly shut. But when the principles of an art form are understood and accorded with, when the rules of training have been well employed as a vehicle in the journey to adeptship, the artist inhabits great freedom of expression. Without those skills so hard-won that freedom is far out of reach, and while we may dress as an artist and brandish the tools of the trade, our artless stumble will trip us up every time.

I attended a concert once, a musical performance by a renowned spiritual master. The concert was to showcase the master's prowess on quite a selection of different musical instruments. Knowing of his skill in various art forms, I was looking forward to a fine musical show. Half an hour into what turned out to be a very long performance I realised the spiritual master didn't have a musical bone in his body. Instrument after instrument did he take up from a revolving table beside him, and he blew and he plucked and he strummed and he drummed forth a startling medley of terrible sounds. I started to think that maybe it was some sort of joke, but as I looked around at the audience assembled there—

comprised largely of devotees of the master—I saw no hint of comedic entertainment, only the rapt attention of the adoring.

Talking to some of them after the show, the devotees explained that it was "transcendental" music we had been treated to, and if it sounded odd it was because we simply could not understand its profundity. Perhaps that is indeed what I witnessed; the principles and practice of music utterly transcended in a joyous and incomprehensible performance. Or perhaps, as it seemed to me at the time, it was merely the fumblings of one whose grasp of the principles—and skill in the practice—of music were meager at best, but which had been rubber-stamped in advance with the seal of mastery by an expectant audience. Mastering something in one realm does not necessarily mean we'll be masters in other arenas. And thumbing our nose at the rules of a discipline probably won't set us free from the shackles of our inability.

The musician spends endless hours playing scales to earn the technical skills and sensitivity required to play their instrument with graceful effortlessness. That expertise, shored up by their understanding of music theory, bestows upon them the freedom to play great music. But that freedom is granted only within the realm of music, and only while the principles of music are being adhered to. To stray from those principles is to abandon the sphere of music and enter the realm of noise-making.[1] And if we take that musician and sit them in front of a canvas with palette and paintbrush in hand but only the principles of music, not painting, to draw upon, we'd better not expect a visual masterpiece.

Nature freely expresses itself, but only through fixed rules; an apple tree performs the miracle of producing fruit, but only successfully gives forth apples, not oranges. Likewise, an artist freely expresses their art, but may only do so by following its rules, with actions based upon its principles.

Rules are the tools used to create the artwork; they are not the artwork itself

Without training, which follows rules, there can be no real freedom to embody the state of effortlessness that artistry provides. Without the sensitivity developed through disciplined training there is no resting in effortlessness, only clumsy forcing that seeks to fit square pegs into round holes. But freedom, of course, is not to be found in the wholesale adherence to rules per se; rules are merely tools we use to build artistry. Blindly clinging to rules gives us no more freedom than never picking them up in the first place.

Once we have reached the point where we have embodied an art form's principles, we no longer need to refer to the rules of training. We rely instead on the indwelling skill and sensitivity that training has built. This is what now informs how we move. We become unconsciously skilled ("unconscious competence," the fourth and final phase of the psychological model known as the four stages of competence[2]), and our constant grasp of a scaffold of rules can relax.

No longer consciously directed to accord with an arbitrary rule-set, our actions arise instead as a spontaneous and appropriate response to the situation at hand. The raw data of this moment is what informs us now; action arises in response to this, to complement this, to fit with this. Such effortless precision is the telltale sign of mastery seen in the improvised play of the musical virtuoso, the casually powerful motions of the martial arts expert, the always perfectly apt and efficient words of the poet. Mastery is skill liberated from the clutches of conscious control. It is not an art form being done by an artist; it is is an art form doing itself.

Such is the goal of we who aspire to grow in the art of living effortlessly; so fully has training established itself that we cannot but fashion fine works of art from the raw material of our lives. But while we are not within sight of that goal we must lay down the law around how we behave; to strengthen those actions that bring us to ease and abandon the ones that tie us in knots.

Training all of life as an art form

The actions that make up our day-to-day lives fall across three realms—those of body, speech and mind. The path of divine laziness, if it is to lead us all the way to freedom and ease, must deal with everything we are able to conjure with our thoughts and our deeds.

Internal activity—all of the varied and colourful behaviour and tendencies of the mind—is most difficult to train. It is subtle and happens at great speed. This is why so many approaches to training the mind begin with practices that first calm and still mental activity, slowing it down to a more manageable speed where the mechanisms in operation can be seen, examined and honed. The discipline of mental development lights up many traditional systems of training. The way of divine laziness glows with it too. We will examine it in some detail later.

The training of our external behaviour—the actions of body or speech, those that impinge upon the world around us—is perhaps more familiar. We're taught from an early age to restrain what we say and do to conform to a set of norms. This training has been useful to allow us to grow as members of society, but is probably rudimentary at best, and might even squash us into unpleasant shapes. To voluntarily set up a scaffold that shapes our doings and sayings more pleasingly can unearth and straighten those unconscious guidelines. It shows us what kinds of actions will trap us or slap us, and helps us avoid them. Dubious actions are put out of reach before we even start reaching for them.

Hosting a code of conduct that can shepherd our external behaviour and keep it from harm's groping hand asks us to roll out the welcome mat for poor old misjudged morality, so reviled and mistrusted by we sophisticated moderns. Morality has inherited a wretched reputation, no doubt due to grievous mishandling of it by the crazed or the cruel or the ignorant. To make it stomachable for those who find it sickening we must paint morality in a new light—in its real light; as a tool for building a thing of great beauty, not a weapon to intimidate others and bludgeon ourselves with. This recasting is attempted in the following chapter.

Through effective training we can develop great freedom in living our lives; not because we carelessly do whatever we want, but because our wants become aligned with what is actually freeing for the heart.

The restraint required to make that alignment can be difficult while blind to the cause and effect relationship between action and result. Small children can't resist reaching for fire, despite their parent's advice, because they don't see the danger. But once our hand has been burned it becomes easy—in fact effortless—to restrain ourselves from putting it back in the fire. We don't even need to think about it because we know, deep down and through first-hand experience, that burning is pain.

So too with the myriad ways we can fashion our lives; a great many modes of conducting ourselves amount to leaping into the flames, and we must bear the blistering results if we take that leap. A regimen that instills in us the sensitivity to notice when we are being burned, the wisdom to realize that burning is to be avoided, and the dexterity to succeed in that avoidance is what we must embark upon if we are to develop the ease and grace of divine laziness, the art of living effortlessly.

Let us, then, set out those proscriptions that steer the enlazening process, and hand ourselves over to them. Far from being a deathgrip that squeezes the life from us, this is the sturdy embrace that holds us in place should we stumble towards the inferno. These rules are the arms that hold divine laziness while still in its infancy and allow it to flourish, and to pulse with the blood of a living path. Can we develop the freedom to live within them?

Chapter Five

Morality: Training External Behaviour

SOME YEARS AGO I was out for an early morning run while staying with friends in Australia. The beautiful surroundings must have stolen my attention, for suddenly I realised my stride had been broken by a deep and unnoticed curb between footpath and road. I'm no acrobat, but in the instant it took for my conscious mind to recognise that the road was rushing up to meet me, my body had already begun to curl itself into a perfect and literally face-saving forward roll.

This body instinctively drew upon a period of training done many years earlier, which involved the diligent practice of forward rolls, often from a runup or a dive. I hadn't done a forward roll in years but somehow knew instantly how to respond when faced with the prospect of hurtling headlong into the gutter. The icing on the cake was that I managed to exit the roll and resume my running stride without missing a beat. It must have looked impressive to those driving by.

The point here is not how cool it is to do impromptu ninja rolls, but how the patient cultivation of a skill can effectively, unconsciously, effortlessly take over and guide our actions in situations where control is lost. Sometimes this can save our skin; without that prior training in forward rolls I'd have been a dead man on that splendid Brisbane morning. It is with this in mind that we turn our attention to the training of our day-to-day conduct along predetermined guidelines, and examine how this training can set us in good stead during times we may find ourselves heading into the gutter.

If we as a society have shunned the notion of laziness, even moreso do we scorn the mere mention of morality. The word makes people cringe. It's laden with misunderstanding and often prompts feelings of guilt and repression, and images of unwanted (perhaps violent) imposition by an external authority. Those who talk of morality do so at risk of being scorned as a puritan. So let's wipe the slate clean and start anew by establishing a clear definition of what morality really means in the context of training in the art of living effortlessly.

Behaviour conducive to wellbeing

Morality, pure and simple, is behaving in a way that is conducive to the wellbeing of others and oneself. It's a stance that cannot be imposed from without but grows in the light of sensitivity, fed by an understanding of cause and effect as it pertains to our actions. In adopting this stance we need to be clear on what we mean by "conducive to the wellbeing of others," for the sentiment has clearly been misused as a means of coercing or forcing others to do what we want of them, "for their own good." How many horrors have been imposed by "well-meaning" reformers who thought they had a better idea of how someone else should be living? More than just an ideology, behaviour conducive to wellbeing must be based upon sensitivity to the effects our actions will have on others, which in turn is based upon an experiential understanding of those effects in our own lives.

By training our hearts and minds through a code of moral discipline we learn to feel directly this cause and effect dynamic; we feel the effects of our actions within our own lives as a direct experience. And feeling those effects in ourselves, we also know how they are likely to feel for others. We know in our hearts when our deeds—whether of body, of speech or of mind—will cause harm to another, because we feel the burn of that harm in ourselves.

Having developed that inner sensitivity it is no longer possible to fool ourselves that cruelty towards someone can possibly be "for their own good." There are cases, of course, where our unintentional actions do cause harm: we step on the cat's tail or smash someone's favourite teacup. But such actions are out of our hands, as it were, and it's important to remember that the intention behind an action is what determines its consequences. We cannot control our every deed, but we can examine our intentions and choose whether or not to act on them.

Moral training

In physical exercise the concept of core strength is celebrated as the foundation upon which all other areas of physical development are layered. The core is the musculature responsible for supporting posture, stability and movement alike, and its development is considered to be of paramount importance in building any kind of physical training regime. Moral training can be thought of as developing the core strength that provides stability for the behavioural system, allowing us to act with poise and effectiveness and keeping in check the more clumsy flailings of our behavioural limbs, and the injuries they cause.

We seem to have a built-in rudimentary moral compass that somewhat guides our behaviour towards wellbeing and away from harm; we probably have enough moral core strength to allow us to go through the motions of life. But refining our conduct beyond those rudiments requires a system of training. And like any system of training it must be based upon rules (see chapter 4). Such a system of guidelines could range from a few simple considerations (such as the golden rule: do unto others as you would have them do to you) to an extremely complex and refined system of rules like those found in certain monastic settings. But to develop in this area one must have a framework.

My own basic framework for moral training has been rooted in the five classical precepts of Buddhism. You may as an exercise spend some time considering for yourself what values you feel are worth preserving and strengthening through training, and formulate your own set of guidelines based upon them. In fact I underwent such an exercise years ago and found at the end of it that my independently arrived at set of precepts were the very same five recommended by the Buddha millennia ago. It seems they are not only built on tradition, but also universal good sense. So let's use them here as a benchmark.

Five precepts

These five basic precepts cover all areas of external action that can cause us misery if left unchecked. Based on the cause-and-effect workings of human activity, they prescribe the minimum standard of behaviour necessary for training ourselves in the art of freeing the heart. Rooted in principles of non-harm, these precepts are undertaken voluntarily as a deliberate limitation upon the range of activities we engage in.

1. I undertake the precept to refrain from killing

2. I undertake the precept to refrain from taking that which is not given

3. I undertake the precept to refrain from sexual misconduct

4. I undertake the precept to refrain from false speech

5. I undertake the precept to refrain from intoxication leading to carelessness

The specific positive-negative way these precepts are presented engages us in *choosing* to *avoid* certain activities, and this is a crucial point: it means they are voluntarily undertaken rather than being imposed by an external authority. It also means they are not necessarily absolutely fixed and inflexible laws; we choose to adhere to them increasingly more as we feel more sharply how painful it is to act outside of them.

These precepts lie as cardinal points on a compass we use to find our bearings. They are a warning system that rings an alarm when we stray. Having determined to live by these rules, that ringing alerts us when we have wandered outside of them. And we notice, if we are sensitive, that actions which deviate from this basic standard have effects felt in the heart that aren't pleasant. That unpleasant residue leaves us disinclined to repeat those actions. We become averse to punishing ourselves. The disinclination to engage in conduct that hurts is the epitome of divine laziness.

Although these precepts are presented in the negative (refraining from certain actions), they each have a positive aspect as well. For example, the precept that swears us off killing also encourages us in its positive sense towards kind and compassionate deeds; refraining from stealing has a positive counterpart in generosity, and so on. These two aspects are sides of the same coin; refraining from causing harm is already alleviating the suffering of others as it removes one harmful person from the world.

Refraining from killing

Of these precepts, this is the most important. It is the foundation that underlies, supports and gives meaning to the others. At its least refined it asks of us only that we do not kill other people. Most of us can agree that not killing one another is a good basic standard for any reasonable human society, and I assume if you're reading this book that murder is not something you're having to hold yourself back from. But as sensitivity grows in our hearts the scope of this precept quite naturally extends far beyond just trying not to take each other's lives.

We develop a distaste for harming others in any way at all and seek to avoid behaviour that is likely to jeopardise another's wellbeing, whether on the coarse level of physical violence, or in more refined realms of emotional torment. We start to notice more acutely the effect our presence has on others and see how an angry expression or belligerent stance casts a shadow over the comfort or ease of those in our vicinity. Perhaps we are able to refine our practice of harmlessness to the point where we are unwilling even to generate violent thoughts towards someone. Who knows what effects if any those thoughts will have on their target, but with sensitivity we feel the uncomfortable residue they leave in our own minds, and the pain of that self-violence is reason enough to keep guard over our inner behaviour. And by the same token, our kindnesses feel just as good to ourselves as to those who receive them.

Let us not forget that we too are the deserving recipients of our own goodwill. Acts of violence towards ourselves—like the way we drive ourselves mercilessly on or crush ourselves under the thumb of obligation—are quite at odds with a precept aimed at minimizing harm. To relinquish harmful behaviour aimed inwards is the first and finest step in disarming our violence towards others.

As this avoidance of harm is developed, a sense of benevolence naturally extends beyond our own species to encompass any and all living creatures—great or small, near or far, dear or annoying. Just as we hold our own lives dearly and want no harm to befall us, so too do other living beings; we all love life and hate pain. Seeing this it's no longer so easy to maintain arbitrary boundaries between species, nor can we continue to pretend the wellbeing of some creatures is worth considering but others don't count.

We sense keenly that destroying the life of any living being or causing them misery and pain is unacceptable. We can no longer delude ourselves that we have the right to decide when and how another being dies. The act of killing drives deeper still the ingrained sense of self-entitlement—the sense of a me that is more important than any you—that sits bloated and ugly at the root of most of our misery. Each fish that we hook, each gnat that we swat is a blow we land upon our innermost face. Let those who have not yet sickened of that self-administered beating continue to hook and swat and smart, but we who prefer a measure less pain would do well to think twice and then thrice before readying the fist.

If we are to grow in divine laziness the stain of violence must be expunged from our hearts. While we choke life in a stranglehold and mete out conduct with a belligerent fist we are never free to relax in the sunlight of laziness, crowded and tormented as we are by the echoes of our brutality. But a life with violence quelled allows that deep rest. The sweetness of a life devoid of violence may only be savoured by one who has put violence away. They alone may describe how delicious it is, while those who still cling to barbary merely lick at the outside of the honeypot, never tasting the nectar within.

Just as we become attuned to the suffering in others by knowing our own, once we have tasted the sweetness of actions that bring joy to others then keeping our intentions anchored in harmlessness is effortless.

Refraining from stealing

Think what a different society we'd live in if everyone abided by just this precept. A world without thieves would mean we'd no longer need to lock our possessions away. Liberated from the tyranny of locks we could walk around free from the burden of jangling bunches of keys. This would indeed be a major step towards a civilised society. (Sorry locksmiths, you'd be out of a job.)

Having been burgled on several occasions, I know well the sense of violation that comes with someone invading our home and making off with our personal effects. And anger too, and indignation; I'd worked hard to obtain those things, only to have a morally crippled intruder run off with them. But I also had occasion to consider the thief's perspective, and it dawned on me how far into foolishness their face had been shoved by their own thieving hands.

Sure, they got away with some stuff (not very good stuff, mind you: a simple man with simple means, I hadn't a great deal to satisfy the greed of a villain), but now they were burdened with that ill-gotten booty, with lugging it to safety then finding someone to sell it to. What a drag. Not to mention the fact that the cops were hot on their trail, and effort and anxiety surely must hound a sought-after criminal. And even these miseries must pale next to the acid that such actions spill in the heart of the doer. I began to pity them (once I'd finished cursing them) and wondered why anyone would bother. If more people were more lazy, I surmised, there would be a dramatic decline in burglaries, as would-be thieves throughout the land realized it was far too much effort for such a pitiful gain.

In a coarse example like that it's easy to see the folly of stealing. But what about the many subtle ways we claim ownership of things that are not really ours? That pirated software on our computers; that jacket which found its way into our hands after somebody left it lying around; the wallet we found in the gutter. In stealing's greyer areas it's easy to explain away our procuring of that which actually belongs to another. After all, those software giants are doing just fine without my registration fee. In fact, aren't they're ripping off honest people like you and me anyway? And what about the old adage: "finders keepers, loser weepers?" Surely that places ownership of someone else's carelessly misplaced belongings squarely in my hands, right?

The answers to questions like these are not to be found in law books or teachings on righteousness, but written here in our hearts. We know when we've let greed or deceitfulness govern our acquisition of a thing, and we feel its results. It's not about being a goody-goody who never does anything wrong, but paying attention to how we relate to the material world and how that relationship feels. How does it feel to appropriate something that we know belongs to another? How does it feel when someones takes something of ours?

Or how about when we return the wallet we found in the gutter to its rightful owner, cash untouched? If the tables were turned we'd hope that the finder would treat us the same. And then if they did, how that would delight us and restore our faith in the goodness of others.

Claiming ownership of something not ours bloats further an already ugly thing: the self-entitlement that tells me I deserve this *at your expense.* That lie is the polar opposite of generosity. It suffocates us in scarcity and drowns us in competition and greed.

The practice of generosity, on the other hand—the positive aspect of this precept—directly undermines greed and develops a sense of community, of cooperation, of all-in-this-together-ness. Thus we celebrate special occasions by the giving of gifts. Giving to others we give to ourselves in ways that are far more lucrative than mere material gain. The gift to ourselves is the whittling away of our greed and possessiveness, of the mad delusion that no matter how much we have, somehow we don't have enough. As that whittling cuts deeper we willingly drop the exhausting travail of trying to extract from a miserly world some meagre trappings with which to furnish our withering lives.

Refraining from sexual misconduct

This precept, while encompassing the way we relate to and indulge in the world of sense-pleasure in general, has its specific focus on sexuality, which has the strongest lure among all the attractions of the sensory world. There is no doubt that sexual energy is a force to be reckoned with. It can create new life from nothing. It can also rip lives apart. In perhaps no other arena of conduct do our greed and selfishness push us about so ruthlessly. People who otherwise stand upright can be bent into crooked and ghastly shapes by the unchecked forces of lust in their bodies and minds. Our deployment of this energy therefore needs to be guarded well and respected for the potent force that it is.

The coarse array of sexual exploitations such as rape, abuse and adultery needs little elaboration here; their injurious effects are all too obvious. But more subtle misuses of sexuality often lie in the way we impose or withhold our sexual attentions. Games of power, domination and manipulation that hold us in their ruinous grip bleed poison into otherwise flourishing relationships. The effect of our sexual activities felt within us speaks of their rotten or loving intent with the voice of pain or delight that cries out in response. And to this voice we must listen, and trust it as a worthy guide in the journey through the pitfalls of life as sexual beings.

Even without a conscious intention to train ourselves with this precept, we find ourselves walled on all sides by laws and conventions that dictate how we should behave in this regard, and with whom. Some of these standards undoubtedly keep us from harm and safeguard the bonds between people that underlie our communities. Some of them do not. And although popular trends or societal taboos have much to say about sexual conduct, they may or may not have any bearing on its actual realities. As always, the guidance we seek here must come from the answer to one question: does this cause harm to myself or another? Only the heart made wise through sensitivity and experience can give a credible answer.

Beyond the realm of sexuality, this precept encompasses the wider sphere of our relationship to sensuality in general. Life in the world is a life of sensual experience. We are hard-wired, it seems, to lean towards experiences we find to be pleasing, and to seek relief from or avoid those that hurt. Training our conduct in the pursuit of these ends is what lies at the heart of this precept. While there is no problem with seeking the pleasant and seeking to be rid of the unpleasant, the means we employ to achieve those ends should accord with our intentions to minimise harm if we are to live at ease.

Those of us who are fortunate enough to have the freedom to do so live in a place that we like; we eat the foods that we find agreeable and dress in clothing that makes us feel good; we spend time with people and engage in activities that bring us happiness and joy. The whole of the human project, with its striving and its ingenuity and its mania for progress, could be summed up as the endeavour to maximise pleasure and minimise pain. The impulse is good, but when it is followed whatever the cost—to the detriment of others or our own wellbeing—we set forth on a course that ruins us. The very actions intended to summon forth our allotment of pleasure, if employed with regard for neither their consequences nor the welfare of those affected, become instead the utensils of pain, and any pleasure they do build is submerged in the silt of the flood of their unwelcome consequences.

With this in mind we learn to examine our impulses towards sensual indulgence. Feeling our wants and desires as they surface, and setting in place some guidelines around how far we allow them to push us around, we learn to hold back where we ought to, seeing that "want" and "must have" are not really the same. As we gain some control over rapacious desires, we see how blind we become when our sights are set on pleasing ourselves. Seeing this blindness renders it null, and so we are able to weigh up the cost of clinging to pleasure, and to slacken our grip when we see it to be too expensive. We fathom the mismatch between short term gain and long term pain, and adjust our efforts to make better use of them.

Refraining from lying

All of us have been lied to. All of us have lied. This precept is impossible to keep if we take it too literally, for the very structure of our social interactions garnishes our conversations with a thousand untruths spoken in ignorance or jest. It is not really these that we're aiming to curb with this precept, but the intentional speaking of untrue words for the purpose of deceiving others, whether for profit, concealment or diversion.

The power of words is considerable—a kind word at the right time can bring light into an otherwise miserable day; a single harsh word said in anger can start a war—and most of us know only too well the pain of discovering we have been lied to. It damages our sense of trust in ways that can take years to recover from, and trust is a cruel thing to deprive someone of, for it is air and sunlight to a growing human heart. To intentionally lie is also to throw away any integrity we might posses; to do so we must first dismantle the foundation of truth upon which we stand. That leaves us on very shaky ground.

In an old story the Buddha outlines to his son Rahula the dangers of lying, comparing by way of simile (as he so often does) a person's integrity to a quantity of water in a bowl. He describes deliberate lying as being like discarding that water and turning the bowl upside down. Just as no water remains in a bowl that's been emptied and turned upside down, so too is there no chance of integrity remaining in someone who lies. Furthermore, he says: "In the same way, Rahula, when anyone feels no shame in telling a deliberate lie, there is no evil, I tell you, he will not do. Thus, Rahula, you should train yourself, 'I will not tell a deliberate lie even in jest.'"[1] Speaking untruths can be seen in this light as a gateway to all manner of unwholesome deeds, for to do so we first cast aside integrity, honour and reverence for truth.

The positive aspect of this precept is, of course, speaking the truth. We make a commitment to truth and are willing to put our mouth where our money is, giving voice to the facts when the situation calls for it. There is, however, the need for some caution here. It seems there's a trend in some circles to "voice your truth" at all costs. But just because something is true does not mean it has to be said. In fact, a great many things that *are* true and *are* said are also terribly harmful to the recipient. Although such speech may technically accord with refrainment from lying, it certainly misses the target of harmlessness. True or not, words spoken with disregard for their impact on others do not qualify as being kind. In such situations it's better to leave that truth unspoken, regardless of whatever notions of "honoring our authenticity" are in vogue.

In this regard it's worth keeping in mind some further advice the Buddha had on speaking truthfully. He suggested four criteria that should be considered before speaking if one is to do so in a profitable way. A word being true is only one part of it being a good thing to say.

- It should be timely. Is this the right time to say this?

- It should be true. Are these the actual facts?

- It should be kind. Is this an uplifting thing to say, or is it cruel?

- It should be beneficial. Are these words profitable or not?[2]

With these four guidelines in mind we can determine whether this truth we're sitting on and so desperate to get out should be offered to the world at all. If all four criteria are met we can sing it out loud, but if not then we might want to store that gem away for another occasion.

Refraining from intoxication

This is perhaps the most controversial of these five moral precepts. The other four explain themselves at a glance, but a bit of assisted merriment? How does that equate to a breach of moral conduct? That is a little less easy to stomach.

This precept suggests avoiding the use of intoxicating substances that retard mental clarity and lead to carelessness. We can think of it as a protective wrapper around the other precepts; it lessens the chance of them being eroded. Intoxicated, we're much more likely to act at odds with our intention to uphold moral conduct: more likely to harm others with ill-considered actions and thoughtless speech; more likely to deform our perceptions around possession and ownership; more likely to make poor choices around sexual activity. This can be easily verified by a trip to a bar late at night.

But it's not just the feckless "eat, drink and be merry" variety of intoxication that this precept encompasses, or even the nightmare of substance abuse and addiction. It cautions against any dulling of mind or blunting of sensitivity, for these are the faculties through which freedom and ease can take shape. Because our training is based on developing clarity of mind and sensitivity of heart, it is wise to steer clear of activities that render those faculties murky. And we muddy the waters through a variety of means.

When I was training as a web developer my tutor quipped that the entire industry runs on caffeine: no coffee, no websites. Coffee and tea are such a ubiquitous part of our culture that we hardly remember they're drugs with actual physical and mental effects. They pick us up and they comfort, and there's certainly nothing wrong with a cup here and there. We love it. But when we start *needing* that fix in order to get through the next meeting, the next chore, the next moment...

This obsessive reworking of our perceptive state, the compulsive rewiring of our interface with life is what we seek to curtail by establishing this precept. Perhaps not especially harmful in the case of coffee or tea, but that tendency to want—to *need*—to change however we are right now so easily gives birth to the habit of intoxication, with all its potential for madness. Examining those tendencies can be enlightening. And having in this precept the cause to do so is a great opportunity.

There is another compulsively-consumed intoxicant that is even more widespread and less questioned: electronic consumption. TV and movies and internet, mobile devices and screens, screens, everywhere screens. They enhance our lives in so many ways. But if we find ourselves slumped on a couch or shambling along with our face in a screen for hours on end while completely ignoring our actual lives, we may want to question our usage.

One of the difficulties with electronic media or any other socially sanctioned drug is the fact that they *are* socially sanctioned. Everyone spends hours on computers or lost in TV, right? The fact that everyone does a thing does not make it a good thing to do. We think nothing of the cozy scene of "family time" around a TV, sharing a room while ignoring each other with all eyes glued to a glowing rectangle. Perhaps that is not so far removed from the vacant-eyed slump of those with a veinful of narcotics, but we find that idea distinctly less cozy.

Is there any real difference between screen-time and narcotic-time? Both see us slack and unplugged from the actuality of our surroundings. Both tend to be quite addictive. Our feelings about the two differ vastly because one of these drugs is socially sanctioned and the other is not.[3] In fact, in some ways you could say that a drug like TV is even more harmful than others, actively bombarding us as it does with an endless stream of covert and explicit garbage about life and the world, and relentlessly telling us we'll always need *something else* to be happy. At least good-old-fashioned regular drugs just leave us with our own nonsense to contend with.

It is not necessarily the substances we use to intoxicate that we ought to eye with wariness, but the drive to resort to such medication in the first place. We all need time out—sometimes a movie or a glass of something is just the ticket—and the art of living effortlessly is partly about relaxing and uncoiling the springs that our lives tend to tighten. But obliterating the faculties of sensitivity and clarity, whatever the means, robs us of the very tools we need to employ in that unwinding.

Does this mean that we can't have a cold beer with a mate on a hot afternoon? Must we shop around for caffeine-free beverages or live in a wifi-free zone? Probably not, and I suspect resorts like that would cause more problems than they would solve. With wisdom and sensitivity we can establish for ourselves the parameters of our relationship with intoxicating substances and practices. It is up to us to answer questions of appropriate use and thresholds of harm, based upon our own experience and informed by sensitivity to their effects in our lives. As with all of these precepts, avoiding something merely because a list tells us to do so, although it may help keep us out of trouble, is not the best way of developing wisdom.

The taking or leaving of intoxicants lies in the realm of external behaviour, but the effects are powerful upon our inner state. While this precept dissuades us from building up an internal tarnish of dullness, its positive aspect is the active polishing of clarity and wakefulness. Practices like meditation (discussed in the following chapter), give us a fine cloth to use in that polishing.

Don't just believe it, try it for yourself

Nothing stinks of inauthenticity more that a set of moralistic rules clung to by one who lacks personal experience of their benefits as well as their limits. A bit of experimentation with these guidelines can greatly enhance our understanding of why they are used. If we are gripped by skepticism or dogmatism we can break a few rules if need be, to feel first hand the results. But a caveat: do it with care. Step outside the container in ways that cause minimal discord. We must ensure the wisdom gained far outweighs any pain incurred in the process. After all, if we want to learn about the effects of heat on the human body we'd hardly go leaping headlong into an inferno. A simple flame would suffice, held at a respectable distance; that is all we'd require to know not to get too close to the fire.

Living within these five precepts goes far beyond merely the passive avoidance of possible avenues of engagement with life. It is an act of great generosity. What we are doing is offering the world a collection of priceless gifts: the gift of someone who gives their fellow beings no reason to fear them; the gift of a person who respects the possessions of others; the gift of someone who does not put their own pleasure before the welfare of those around them; the gift of a speaker of truth, one who does not seek to deceive; the gift of a person who prizes clarity and sensitivity, and won't scatter harm about in a daze. The value of such gifts is not to be underestimated.

Removing detrimental options from our range of possible actions greatly simplifies our lives, making it much easier to know what to do. The foolishness of morally questionable behaviour is no longer seen as a viable option. The vegetarian at a restaurant offering only one or two suitable options has a far easier time of it than the poor old omnivores, obliged as they are to deliberate over the abundance of meaty dishes on offer. In the same way, those who have written off ruinous deeds as unfit for consumption don't give them a second glance, and don't miss the heartburn they bring. When most of our options are poison but some are delicious and wholesome the choice is an easy one. If we can tell the difference.

As wisdom has more of a say in the choice of our deeds we realize that picking up some things is far more effort—and far less rewarding—than simply leaving them be. We grow sick of having to drag around a heart stained with guilt, streaked with remorse, heavy with regret for the rest of the day, the week, a lifetime. We have become too lazy for that, and that laziness is divine.

Moral restraint is not a cage that imprisons. The heart burnished by moral integrity is truly free do what it wants, because all it wants is that which is freeing.

Chapter Six

Meditation: Training Internal Behaviour

HAVING SET UP A means of restricting external behaviour that tends to callus the heart, we now turn attention toward the training of our internal behaviour—that of the mind itself. Here we approach the task of establishing effortlessness and sensitivity right where our actions originate. We embark upon the enlazening of the mind.

Much has been said about freeing ourselves from suffering through training the mind, and a strikingly clear voice in this dialogue is that of the Buddha. For forty years he walked the land teaching that very thing to those with ears to hear. That was over two and a half thousand years ago, but still the message echoes on and has never been more relevant. Some of that vast monument of wisdom found its way into a collection of sayings in verse form, which opens with the following stanzas:

> Mind is the forerunner of all actions.
> All deeds are created by mind, led by mind.
> If one speaks or acts with a corrupt mind,
> Suffering follows,
> As the wheel follows the hoof of an ox pulling a
> cart.

> Mind is the forerunner of all actions.
> All deeds are created by mind, led by mind.
> If one speaks or acts with a serene mind,
> Happiness follows,
> As surely as one's shadow.[1]

Seeing that "all deeds are created by mind, led by mind," it is clear that training the mind is the best way to shape how we act.

Bridging the chasm between a corrupt mind that drags misery in its wake and a mind that is serene and beams happiness is the aim of the art of living effortlessly. That means finding, uncovering and walking a path of training that leads up to and over that bridge. The practice of meditation serves the wayfarer well in this regard, paving that path with vitality and sweeping it clear of danger and debris.

Although this chapter is not intended as a training manual for meditation—for that kind of guidance I suggest seeking out a genuine teacher—it does present an overview of some core principles that underpin many meditative paths and practices. Meditation has long been employed, in one form or another, by those looking to free themselves from the grip of mental captivity and bewilderment and emerge into the freedom of truth. Principles and practices of various methods aimed at this have been preserved through the ages, safeguarded by the world's great mystical traditions. And although the particulars of technique and cosmology may vary from case to case, all have at their heart a simple aim: tuning the mind so that truth can be seen and reality known.

My own experience and training in meditation has taken place mainly within a Buddhist context, that being the tradition which called me to this path and equipped me for its rigours. Therefore my frame of reference when approaching meditation is primarily a Buddhist one, and the principles examined here are essentially those of the form known as insight meditation. You may approach meditation through a different tradition, or no tradition at all. It doesn't really matter. Regardless of setting, the aim is the same: training the mind to see the truth.

When employed with sincerity and polished with patient care this practice may lead us right up to the face of consciousness itself, even beyond, as mystics through the ages have always attested. The odyssey begins not with fanfare but a quiet turning inward and a willingness to see what it's like to just stop.

Long ago, back near the start, I was told: "Meditation is not about getting some particular experience. It's about understanding the nature of experience itself." That is, the particular experiences one has along the way are not nearly so important as the understanding developed in the process. It is the growth of this understanding that is the real value of having a meditation practice in one's life.

For our purposes here—the training of the mind in the art of divine laziness; the fostering there of effortlessness and sensitivity; the enlazening of the mind, if you will—we can think of the meditative process as consisting of three distinct facets. First, the stilling of the mind through focused attention, which brings about clarity and allows for the body and mind to settle and relax at many levels. Second, using the stillness and clarity thus established, we carry out an investigation of experiences as they come and go in awareness. Simply watching as the manifold contents of awareness rise and fall, we begin to see and understand their nature. Third, as understanding of the nature of experiences takes root, and as some of their tricks are revealed, our fascination with them starts to dim and we develop a taste for simply abiding as the knowing of experience. Or, simply being. These three facets we can think of as stilling, seeing and being.

Stilling

Stilling the mind is vital to its training and the gateway to the practice of meditation; it allows clear seeing to happen. Once again we find an illuminating analogy in water, which in its natural and unperturbed state is clear and calm. A still pool is naturally clear, and we can see right to the bottom with ease. We can see, shall we say, right to the heart of it. When a breeze ripples the surface of the pool, however, its transparency lessens and we can no longer so easily see to the depths. Throw in a rock and the splash lets us see even less. Fill the pool with thrashing piranhas and visibility drops close to nil. The mind is like this: while it boils with emotion or seethes with ideas there is little chance of seeing what lies in the deep. But when still and settled there is no end to the clarity.

Taking the analogy a little bit further we can look at water's capacity for reflection. Upon the surface of a still pool appears the face of one who peers into its depths, reflected as in a mirror. All that is required is a shift of visual focus to see our face looking back at us. The still mind, too, has this reflective quality, a quality not available when turbulence reigns.

This is why the practice of meditation always begins with stopping and stillness. Physical stillness comes first; we stop moving and keep the body still. We adopt a position that allows for comfort and disinclines us to fidget. A motionless body prepares a seat for the mind to sink into quietude. Even in meditative practices that do require motion, such as tai chi or sufi whirling, movements are curtailed to be simple and few, deliberate and calculated; stillness in motion if you will.

This simple practice in itself—the bodily shift from movement to stillness, from complexity to simplicity, from doing to none—is already enough to begin melting layers of tension clutched in our bodies. The fists of a lifetime of strain are allowed to unclench; knots of anxiety untie. Even this much, though only the start, is already a major advance down the pathway to ease. This physical stillness certainly predisposes the mind to slow down as well, but by no means is it guaranteed. For that we employ the primary tool of the meditative procedure: focused attention.

Our ability to bring our attention to an object of choice is what allows us to perform the various mental tasks required of us in daily life. (Some have said that this is the only control we really have—the ability to decide where we place our attention. Who am I to say otherwise?) This bringing of attention is the preliminary step in the practice of calming the mind, but it is the act of holding attention on that object for extended periods that allows the mind to settle and become still. This is the experience of anyone who has been engaged in intense mental focus for some purpose—solving a mathematical problem, composing a piece of music, playing a video game—all other considerations vanish from view leaving only that one object of concentration. When we do this intentionally and systematically we come to experience first hand how the mind settles and becomes still, mental activity slowing to a halt as a solitary object takes the entire stage.

Like any skill, this takes time to develop, and early attempts are anything but that simple. In fact, it is the common experience of most for the mind to seem to become even *more* hectic and hyperactive when a first deliberate attempt at calmness is made. Actually, this is just the result of finally being able to see, through the bringing of attention, just how busy and unruly our minds really are. Mostly we don't notice the babble that fills our minds continuously, engaged as we are in some tangent or adrift in currents of thought or fantasy. But when we stop and finally look, the mess we behold! Previously unnoticed mental debris is seen to fill the mindscape from horizon to horizon, an asteroid field bombarding itself in a riot of chaos. But if, undeterred, we keep coming back to the training ground we may nurture an ability to sustain attention on a single stabilizing point.

It doesn't so much matter what the object of attention is. It could be a candle, a vision, a phrase, the touch of our feet on the ground as we walk; each would suffice as a hitching post to which we may tether our focus. The breath is the most common, though, mainly due to the fact that it's always available. The day we don't have a breath to focus on is the day we won't need to anyway. Therefore many are the meditative paths that begin with the simple instructions to "sit down, close your eyes, come to breath." In keeping with this heritage let us, in this example, assume for our object that same tried and tested utensil.

We bring our attention to the breath—in...out...in...out—and we hold it there as long as we can. By and by the mind wanders off. As soon as we notice we collect it and bring it back to the breath—in...out...in...out—and we hold it there as long as we can. And soon, so soon, the mind is besieged by its wanderlust again. So again we bring it back, and again, and again, and this is the practice, this is the task. Once we notice we've lost it again, we simply and gently bring it back. Like a muscle we build through lifting a weight, like a cure we effect through frequent care, like a treasure we polish from dullness to shine, through this training we strengthen both our capacity to sustain attention and our ability to notice when we've strayed from the path into byways of ideation.

Steadily, gradually, there grows a measure of jurisdiction over the irksome antics of a wayward monkey of a mind. And this is the edge that lets us have more of a say in how we behave, that gives us more of a hand in guiding those actions that are "created by mind, led by mind." Then maybe not so much suffering will follow us around like a cart behind an ox.

Developing these liberating skills—the ability to focus our attention and to notice when our minds are astray—is therefore a step towards unshouldering the burden of a future choked with the painful consequences of poorly chosen behaviour. For, as we examined in chapter two, present actions determine the future; poor quality actions done now send an unfavourable stain spreading through whatever comes next.

As meditators with diverse temperaments we develop in these ways at varying rates according to our lot. But eventually, with practice, we may indeed notice that our experience of meditation is punctuated by periods where the mind becomes calm and still, periods where the main impression is one of great silence, periods imbued with upsurges of the corroborative markers of stillness: joy and bliss.

So now what? The mind becomes still—all well and good—but for what? For many, this is the sum and substance of meditation practice: calming the mind to allow tranquility to arise. And as great as that is, surely it's not an end in itself, for recall the aphorism: "Meditation is not about getting some particular experience. It's about understanding the nature of experience itself." And so it is. Although stillness of mind does foster a range of powerfully beneficial effects at all levels of the person, and acquaints us with some of the deeper riches of mind such as joy, bliss and clarity, its main virtue goes far further. Stillness is just the first step, a tool that we've patiently fashioned and sharpened through practice, a tool that should now be put to good use.

The theater of the tranquil mind sets the stage for deep investigation, allowing us to see clearly how the mind operates. It allows us to see things as they actually are. This is the aspect of meditation that we may call seeing, and the beam of awareness born of a still and focused mind can burn like a laser through cataracts that get in the way.

Seeing

The great meditation master Ajahn Chah[2] was often approached by people seeking advice, and such an inquirer one day asked how much calm it is necessary to cultivate. He answered, in his characteristically pragmatic style, that "enough" calm is required. Enough for what? Enough to allow investigation to happen, for insight to get its foot in the door. Our "normal" mind state of agitation and animation is unsuitable for investigating the nature of experience itself. But once a reasonable degree of stillness is present we can put our minds to just that use.

As we bring the clarity born of a tranquil mind to bear on our experience, attending to it closely and analyzing its innards, its real nature and workings may be observed. The mind is seen as a stage, a theater, our experiences cast as all manner of characters who enter, act out their drama then leave with a boo or a bow. The practice of seeing avoids becoming entangled in these performances or enamoured of their charm, and simply watches as they go through their steps. Anything that is happening—physical sensations, pleasure and pain, the sensory experiences taken as sight, sound, smell, taste or touch, thoughts and feelings, perceptions or mental tendencies—all of these can be viewed in this way; simply seen as they come and then go.

Normally, as experiences unfold, we're bewitched by our assumption they're real and substantial, and imbue them with a gravity they do not deserve. We find ourselves right there on the stage, engaged in the melodrama. Such is the skill of these cunning thespians: they have us believing the plot is real. But through sitting back and simply seeing—declining, in the spirit of divine laziness, to drag ourselves into the farce—we come to discern some very important things. This discernment can shatter illusions and cast the yoke of blind compulsion from our shoulders. It can change our relationship with experience forever.

First and foremost among these insights is the realization that all experiences are impermanent. We've known this all along at some level, I suppose, but the direct seeing of this in actual experiences as they come and go moment to moment is a revolution in our relationship with these transient wayfarers. Whatever events are occurring—be they of body or mind, pleasant or painful, of long duration or over in a flash—they all follow the same basic pattern: they arise, they persist for some time, and then they come to an end.

There are no exceptions. It is impossible to find a set of conditions that didn't begin and won't end. By attending closely to our experience we can verify this for ourselves. We watch, time and again, as everything that occurs to us follows that same predictable routine. Arise, linger, decline. Start, middle, end. Come, change, go. Purposefully noting this process again and again through our practice of meditation has the effect of releasing us from the assumption that experiences be taken absolutely seriously, and that I must have the "right" ones and crush the "wrong" ones from my life. The evidence that none of it lasts has the power to uproot those assumptions.

This practice of seeing passes no judgment on the actual contents of the experiences that arise and depart. Good, bad or boring, it makes no difference at all to the seeing that seeks to understand them, like the sun who has nothing to say about the quality of the worlds it sheds light upon. And those worlds may not be ones we would wish to inhabit.

When I first learned to meditate I set about it with gusto. A strictly cross-legged affair it was for me; no other posture would do. By confining myself to lengthening periods in this pose I invited the inevitable but unwelcome reward for my zeal in the form of a swollen knee. Beset by this painful knee (a common experience, as it turns out, for one who tries to contort for too long), I would find myself in the grip of complaints: "Not this again. Why does this always happen? I don't deserve it. This has to go so I can get on with my meditation." But of course such lamentation bears no useful fruit. It only strengthens the tendency to complain about discomfort.

Rather than adding to that uninspiring litany of objections, we can simply watch the pain as it takes up residence in that knee; we follow it as it goes through changes in location, as it transforms its shape and intensity. We touch it with awareness right to the end, studying it from every angle: what is this pain anyway? It's surely not inherent to the knee, for it wasn't there before sitting down. But here it is, for better or worse, so why not get to know it a little better?

When we extend our hospitality to an experience and welcome it in for a time it tells us all about itself and, if we're paying attention, it teaches us secrets and departs as a friend. We can play the welcoming (or at least tolerant) host to all of our experiences, becoming well-versed in their variety and knowledgeable as to their natures. We needn't damn and hate the painful ones or beg them to leave us alone. Nor must we lust after pleasant ones, sucking their sweetness and clutching them to us. The understanding born through letting them be, letting them come and letting them go, reveals their nature as changeable ghosts and frees us from servitude to them. This familiarity with our mental activities equips us well for the task of their conscious government, the task which our training in divine laziness charges us with.

Seeing experiences in their true guise—as devoid of permanence and therefore of any real substance or certainty—no longer do we lavish blind faith upon them. No longer do they hold us in their mesmerizing thrall. Like a magician who holds us under his spell while his sleight of hand beguiles us but whose tricks lose their power when we know the mechanism behind them, our experiences no longer bewitch us so well once we've toured backstage and seen them for the cardboard cutouts they are. The illusion is shattered.

And if, throughout this process of simple seeing, we eschew all impulses to change what is happening, and instead simply allow what is happening to happen as it will, we strengthen the sinews of non-doing that hold us steady and at ease as our habits command us to struggle against the unwanted. We develop a taste for just sitting still and allowing a thing to unfold as it will. We learn to relish the beauty of letting things take their course, and see clearly that much of what our jittery impulses would bid us commit is entirely unnecessary—perhaps even harmful. We start to lose faith in the half-baked advice of those impulses, and demote them from ministers to minor advisers.

And so, as we quietly bear witness to all that passes through our meditative milieu, we remain unmoved and unmoving, even amidst the clamouring voices of habit and whim. As experiences rise and fall we hold our stance and look on. This is the effort (for it can be an effort to stay unmoved and aloof as habitual impulses push us and pull us and kick up a fuss) that results in effortlessness, like the digging and sowing that readies the garden so we may laze in the sun while nature produces our crops.

We train ourselves directly and deeply to shy away from doing where doing will do us no good; thus we abide in the right kind of laziness. Our efforts are efforts that bring about effortlessness, our doings the doings that lead to non-doing.

This process refines our sensitivity at a deep and fine level—the level of impulse and intention—and digs potent fertilizer into the soil of our behavioural landscape. The crop such well-prepared soil can yield is effortlessness of a rich and nourishing strain. The mind that has learned to feel into a moment before deciding how or whether to act, that is a mind well suited to govern the behaviour of one who seeks to live free of the harrowing consequences that snap at the heels of blind and unskillful activity.

As the mind is thus cultivated through a formatted practice of meditation, its effects can increasingly be seen to spill out into day-to-day life as well (which is, of course, the whole idea). Removed, though, from the supportive structure of physical stillness and quietude, our reactions to things during workaday life can be far more tricky to deal with. These reactions are often so automatic and pre-programmed that we fail to see them as they are: not accurate indicators of reality but arbitrary sets of pre-packaged reactions, driven by the three hidden roots that give sustenance to the entire family of ill-aimed actions. Greed. Aversion. Delusion. These three, as we saw in chapter one, lie waiting at the dawn of our actions, set poised to poison our behaviour should the cracks in attention become wide enough for them to come slithering through. As we bring the tools of stilling and seeing to bear on everyday situations, we time and again get to see how actions are fed by these roots.

Imagine, for example, we're enjoying a bus ride. Rather pleasant really, as we roll through the streets, until a group of loudmouths climb aboard, all high-volume and low-brow: annoying! Such impositions can well give rise to aversion, and we cringe away from the irritation as our thoughts turn to daggers. How dare they ruin a perfectly good trip with their nonsense? Can't these people see there are others here to consider? But the task of the meditator is not to construct elaborate theses on why everything is wrong. It is to bring attention, directly and purposefully, to what is happening—in this case the process of aversion as it manifests in this body and mind. We feel the slap of annoyance throw a frown across our face. We feel the fist of frustration as it squeezes our guts, as it paints our thoughts red. We feel how we writhe in distaste, leaning forward to a future that breathes a sigh of relief as "our" bus empties out and peace reigns once again. And... that's all. We just feel it.

We just watch it erupt on the scene in all its dull glory, we hold it in awareness as it squirms through our being. And we watch it subside, for surely it will; nothing that comes doesn't go. We don't have to like the situation we're in, but we don't have to leap down the throat of aversion either. We needn't condemn ourselves yet again to a sentence of hating the way things are. The path we tread here is the middle way, steering clear of the extremes of expression and suppression. To express this aversion—to unleash a tirade of abuse at the objects of our displeasure, or to sit steaming and fuming, pouring curses and bile through our veins—would be miserable. And to suppress this aversion, to pretend it's not there or to reason it away—because a wise and compassionate meditator like me shouldn't get angry about things like this, right?—would likewise not serve us so well.

There is a middle way between these two, and that is awareness. To receive the actuality of what is happening—in this case, the fact that we've become enraged by some jabberers—and to allow it to happen fully without either inciting it to explode or suffocating it into silence, to simply watch the aversion unfold in its primary colours and burn itself out when it's done, that is the practice of seeing.

The same holds true for the grip of greed too. The body informs us that something's afoot, that wanting has entered the scene. The mind now inflamed reaches out in desire, insisting we fill its demands with a grab. We don't have to act; we always can choose to opt out, to give up, but only if we see clearly what's happening. We also don't have to tell ourselves off for our greed, our aversion, our delusion. If they're here, they're here, and piling more hatred on top of them only deepens the quicksand. We note what is happening, resting attention on body and mind as they play host to the comings and goings.

And so, as each new harangue is driven our way, we walk the path that neither gets sucked into it nor pushes it away. And as it lives out its short life within us we watch, we wait, and most of all we learn to let it go.

Let It Go

Ajahn Chah once famously said: "If you let go a little you a will have a little peace; if you let go a lot you will have a lot of peace; if you let go completely you will have complete peace." When put like that it's obvious what we need to do, but it's not so easy to embody.

The praise for peace is on plenty of lips, but too often our agent for letting go is a wolf in saint's clothing, amounting to little more than pushing away that which we don't want, rejecting the parts of experience we'd rather not be having. Disguised as letting go, this subtle get-lost is mistaken for truly relinquishing our deathgrip on getting what we want. Such a rejection is, of course, nothing but more of the same old aversion, despite its seductive whispers about letting it go.

To gain a truer understanding of this three-word refrain—let it go—we can apply the tools of reductionism and dismantle it into its parts, and analyze each. Thus an understanding of the whole may be gained through an appreciation of its components. Laying emphasis on each word in turn, let's see if we emerge with an image, vivid and clear, of what it (really) means to let go.

- *Let* it go. The emphasis here is on "let." We allow, we permit, we relinquish control. In the same way that we "let" tea brew in the pot, or "let" someone else drive our car, we harbour no designs on the process other than releasing our grip. Once that grip is relaxed, we need not then push it away. Pushing is not letting, as those who've tried hurrying a cat out a door will know. Having rightly seen that the responsibility of control lies elsewhere, we rest free of investment in the going of the thing. To let is to acknowledge that it is, truly, out of our hands.

- Let *it* go. We emphasize "it" and take ourselves out of the process. It will go in its own good time; it may take long or it may be soon, but go it certainly will. Faith in the process is paramount here, the faith that comes through having seen first hand how everything goes in the end. By relegating it and not us to the doer's seat we release ourselves from the role of the pusher. We do ourselves out of a job, a job whose wages are tension and tears. We're not holding on but nor are we throwing away. We don't have to: it will go of its own accord, and we are letting it do so.

- Let it _go_. Highlighting "go" we acknowledge the fact that it will leave us alone. It is in the nature of all things to slide into the haze, to see out their time then decline. The process of a thing's going may not always happen the way we would want, but in letting it go we allow it to do so on its own terms. Any tampering from us and we're back in the game of pushing away.

Putting these parts back together, the process of letting it go is seen to be a passive affair. Rather than thrusting away that which is distasteful to us—which is nothing more than our same old strategy of control and aversion that has always brought such miserable results—we stop holding on by simply releasing our grip, then watch as the rest just happens. True letting go forms the sinews that shore up the backbone of a life of freedom and ease. Let go a little, little peace. Let go a lot, big peace. Let go completely...

Such letting go is made possible in a mind prepared by a path of meditation. And when through stilling we pause in our frantic clamber up the jagged rock face of ceaseless activity; when, through seeing, the rock face itself is shown up as the phantom it always has been; then the hooked and bloodied fingers of clinging let go in relief and at last we fall back into the embrace of bottomless being.

Being

We've heard it a thousand times: you can't be something you are not. And true it is, for we can only be what we already are. Through stilling and seeing we come to understand that the contents of awareness—the sensory experiences, bodily feelings, thoughts, ideas and beliefs, "the full catastrophe" as Zorba the Greek might put it—do not and can never define what we are; they come out of nothing and vanish completely. We also see that while all things come and go, the knowing of that remains constant and is unchanged, unperturbed by any of it. What we are, if anything, is that knowing. And where we can rest, if anywhere, is right here as that.

This simple repose as the world comes and goes is the resting that we can call being. Here in the eye of the storm it is calm, while all around is aswirl. There's nothing to do and nowhere to go. We are what we've been all along: no-one, going nowhere, doing nothing. This is ultimate laziness: disengaged completely from doing anything at all, though plenty is being done; acutely sensitive to every coming and going. Non-doing, before doing even takes shape. Non-resisting before resistance even takes form. Effortlessness before effort is born.

Being is the great non-doing at the heart of divine laziness, the letting-be of the world as it rises and falls within us. And so our decree "don't just do something—sit there!" finds its truest expression. We leave it all alone, but with interest and care, the way a parent might watch a small child at play. We don't spoil the game by imposing our preferences. We just delight in its wild and spontaneous unfolding.

And if we should notice that action is called for we rouse ourselves up into doing, counseled by the illumination of seeing, refreshed by the restorative draught of being. Doing is then a matter of choice—a deliberate action in response to a need—not the automated fiddling of the anxious or domineering. Efficient and effective, this kind of doing is cleaner by far than the wasteful convulsions of "normal" habit-driven activity. And so our behaviour, corralled from without by the container of moral training which keeps us from courting disaster, is also attuned from within by a heart that is learning directly and deeply to let go of what doesn't matter. The ear becomes tuned to the great silence underlying the noise of our world as it rattles and shouts. More and more we get a taste for this silence and turn to rest in it as the knowing.

The practice of meditation is the mortar that gives strength and stability to the house of divine laziness, a house in which we can truly be at ease. It is the whetstone that sharpens our sensitivity to the currents and clues of this moment. And when our training in the art of living effortlessly draws its sap from the level of being, how richly it can flourish, nourished by the sanity there. An art form fed on such nectar may grow very far indeed, perhaps all the way to mastery.

Chapter Seven

Mastery

SUPPOSE WE HAVE SEEN that life has been crammed with layer upon layer of needless activity.

Suppose we've begun to feel into things, to touch their shape and taste what they're made of.

Suppose we've grown tired of resisting the way it all flows and prefer to go with it instead, but steering it well with the hand of the heart we avoid a collision with woe and seek out a more profitable course.

Suppose we now dwell within the boundaries of a well-considered training that sculpts our behaviour and brightens our mind, guided by rules that keep us afloat in a deluge of doing.

Suppose, then, we are walking the way of artistry, and each step we take brings us closer to freedom and further away from the dullness that blinds and the clumsiness that batters our love and bruises our life. This way may be long, and no-one would call it easy, but ease is its aim and ease is its end. And, once at the end, the rules of the road may no longer dictate our behaviour, for there we may find a more expedient manual: the arcanum of nature itself.

One who has trained long and well at their craft may look about and find themselves in a fresh landscape. Landmarks once depended upon for our bearings have been left behind; no longer is conscious reference to the rules or principles of the art required when we act, for our actions accord with them spontaneously, directed by the situation at hand, ever appropriate. Now the rules of training that guided us inwards to the heart of our art form have taken root in our being and sculpted the shape of our faculty of doing. The principles that scaffold the art have sunk in and become embodied, become enminded. Habits hard won through long training have become second nature. In fact, they have become first nature. These well-trained habits are now the first response to a situation, prior to thought and without deliberation. The way of the art form itself is the master's primary course of action.

A pathless land

If the truth has been called a pathless land, the state of mastery is that very same kingdom, for the master is one who has won to the truth of their art form and gives it a shape. And pathless that mastery it is, not because it cannot be traversed, but because it favours no particular path; every which way is open, and any direction is viable, for the great hallmark of mastery is freedom. We walk the narrow path until the path runs out, and then we place our faith in our well-trained steps to take us where they will.

Here no predefined set of rules prescribes how to be and how to behave; the terrain itself dictates where we go, and how. We do as we see fit, but the ingrained methods of response that our training has equipped us with have put safely out of reach those actions that would lead to disaster. The master tightrope walker won't take a misstep and plummet to the doom that surely awaits down below; the body simply will not let that happen, so tuned is it to the way it must move to stay balanced and aloft. The master poet will never misuse words or throw them together distastefully, but effortlessly crafts from unlimited options the perfect composition that captures a fragment of life and presents it as a thing of beauty. The greatest musician stands out of the way as the right notes flow through, shaped by and shaping the contours of the music.

In the same way, one who has followed the path of divine laziness beyond the districts of conscious development may find themselves under a safeguard. Sensitivity and effortlessness now take over at the helm: they form bulwarks that keep us out of the glue of ruinous conduct; they prompt us with just the right lines to enrich our engagement with life in a way that is heartening.

Inadvertent mastery

The province of mastery is not so exotic as we may believe. Many of us have mastered various aspects of our daily lives merely through the course of living them. Perhaps we have arrived at mastery of walking; we give it not a thought as we nimbly leap over obstacles or quick-step through a crowded street, our stride adjusting and readjusting instinctively while our conscious attention is elsewhere. Perhaps we have arrived at mastery of talking; speech flows, guided by the subject at hand, the right words ready with no need to rummage, the wrong ones bitten back before they get a chance to spoil or offend. Perhaps we have mastered the reading of social cues; the tone in a room is felt and accorded with instantly as we enter; we subtly respond to the mood of the group, building rapport, establishing empathy. Or perhaps we've just mastered the getting of food to face without making a mess. (Or perhaps we have not.)

If so, these things are done effortlessly—without us, despite us—with a fluency that bears the fingerprints of mastery. These are the results of numberless hours of training—undertaken inadvertently as inescapable parts of the daily round of our lives—which builds in us the sensitivity to act with the effortlessness of natural, unscheduled behaviour. If such mastery can happen unbidden, unwittingly, how much more so when we seek it and feed it and nurture it lovingly? How much more fruitful to walk on a path recommended to us by those who have been to where it runs out and can vouch for the riches found there?

Pathless path

When we train in an art form we do so with an eye on the goal of its mastery. And we do so inspired by the masters we meet, or the masters we hear of; those whose tales have been passed on as cultural treasures, as torches that light up the way leading out of the doldrums of mediocrity. For when we see in mediocrity the same numbness, the habitual doing, the same sheer laziness that holds our noses to the grindstone of worry and woe, how gladly we follow that torch. We set out on such training with the keenness of one who eagerly puts down a burden long shouldered.

> Let the dread of endless mediocrity
> spur you into great effort,
> like a well-trained horse
> encouraged by the mere touch of the whip.

> Relinquish the burden of endless struggle
> with unapologetic confidence,
> with purity of action, effort, concentration,
> and by conscious and disciplined
> commitment to the path. [1]

So let that great effort be the effort that commits us to the art of living effortlessly. Let us, through great sensitivity, feel the touch of the whip and the spur that reminds us this is an art form worth striving to master. Let us follow the signposts that point to divine laziness, treading that path till the path runs out, then trusting in sensitivity and effortless instinct to take us from there.

In the pathless land of mastery one is free to move about at will, for conscious training has established the principles of our art form as instincts that deftly keep us from danger, while guiding our steps in a dance that is danced with the comings and goings of now as it waxes and wanes. Forget the map of what to do, and when. "Ultimately," said Morihei Ueshiba, founding master of Aikido, "you must forget about technique. The further you progress, the fewer techniques there are. The Great Path is really No Path."[2] Those on that Great No Path no longer care for specific tricks or techniques that fit only certain scenarios. The days of collecting utensils are gone, for in the state of mastery it is sensitivity, coupled with a body-mind perfectly tuned, that is relied upon.

The rules of training are useful—necessary—but they are just that: rules of training. They bring our actions into tune with the principles that underlie the art. But once those principles have sunk deep enough, the training rules that instilled them can well be discarded as no longer relevant. What informs our actions now is a natural response to the requirements of the moment, and the architecture of that response cannot be set in stone, for its foundations and materials shift as each moment changes and flows.

Neither logic nor planning make up the cement that fortifies masterful action and holds together the path of No Path; it is sensitivity, and a lifetime of training in how to behave and respond.

The principles of the art form being lived are the fingers and thumb of the hand of nature itself, the hand that guides the master's behaviour. As the character of that guiding hand is known more deeply and dearly, its fingerprints may be noticed all over the whole of creation. The master is one who aligns with its doings and so their actions are effortless and fit for the present conditions. While we do not act with mastery, our efforts are crude and half-baked; the hand of nature is thwarted at every step by our clumsy insistence on doing it badly. The road to mastery is learning to feel the way that hand works and to work with it. The path of the master, which is no-path, is doing with that hand, which is no-doing.

> The Art of Peace originates with the flow of things —its heart is like the movement of the wind and waves. The Way is like the veins that circulate blood through our bodies, following the natural flow of the life force. If you are separated in the slightest from that divine essence, you are far off the path.[3]

And this flow of things is ultimately what does any doing that appears to be done by the master. Illustrating this in the context of wing chun my sifu is fond of paraphrasing Bruce Lee: "Forget about hitting, you won't need to. When the time is right, 'it' hits all by itself." Mastery is simply being attentive and being ready, with a well-honed set of faculties, so "it" can "hit" when the opportunity arises. And that may look quite different from what we expect.

One who has mastered an art form can seem to subvert its rules at times, to go against everything they teach. But this is only a phantom duplicity; far from flouting their art form, the master's actions are congruous indeed with its principles, but at a level far deeper than that of the rule-bound apprentice. That congruity is with the movements of nature itself in this moment; it accords with that first, and the rules of the training ground second.

Many's the fool who's mistakenly charged a master with hypocrisy, mouth full of denouncements while waving the rulebook but empty of the understanding that would see masterful action for what it is. But those who chance to recognise mastery when it hits them in the face take no umbrage that their conventional world has been undermined. Rather they feel it as the goad of inspiration, a touch of the whip and the spur, and double their efforts.

When I first began training in wing chun the instructions for doing a given technique were very clear and specific. Each must be done exactly like so, with elbow here, wrist there, all angles of limbs in relation to body exactly controlled. No deviation allowed, techniques that were off by an inch would be frowned on as wrong. The instructions were always the same: meticulous, pedantic; and so the techniques were learned, and so they were trained, time after time after time.

But when I'd observe the masterful ones, their techniques were done with a different agenda. When no longer done as a stationary and solo performance but as part of a moving interplay between two participants, myriad conditions inform how the technique is utilized. Its shape and usage depend on what's happening, over and above the rigorous rules that governed its growth. The principles of the technique hold fast, but the rules that govern its execution are built by the many other energies at play and must shift and flex accordingly. The technique is not a stand-alone thing but part of an integral whole composed of many moving parts. The static rules that defined it so crisply at first no longer suffice. The masterful ones are alive to the moment, fitting in to the moment, not demanding that the moment fits itself to some stagnant and unresponsive standard.

For the master, no longer is there much concern for using correct techniques; far more important is making the right move. Their command of their art form has set them at ease because every move is a right one, and their well-tended instincts won't let them go wrong.

A story from a dear friend of mine, who trained for years as a Buddhist monk, captures well the perplexing difference between master and neophyte. The story concerns my friend's teacher, and takes place back when that teacher was only a novice, newly-ordained and living in Thailand with *his* teacher, the renowned master Ajahn Chah.

Every morning the monks would go out on alms-round to the villages near the monastery to collect their daily allotment of food, as has been the custom for Buddhist monks since the beginning. Ajahn Chah, being the abbot and most senior monk, would walk at the front of the line, with the others arranged in descending order of seniority behind him, as dictated by the conventions of monastic training. On one particular outing, my friend's teacher noticed the relaxed manner of Ajahn Chah; the way he seemed to be so comfortable in his own skin, and indeed in his own robes, as he was wearing them in a fairly loose and casual fashion. The rules of monastic training encourage monks to be very particular with how they present themselves, especially when outside monastery grounds, which creates a favourable impression upon onlookers but can also lead to varying degrees of uptightness around how robes should be worn. Impressed by Ajahn Chah's seemingly nonchalant approach my friend's teacher decided to mimic him, draping his own robes in a lackadaisical manner, casually tossed over one shoulder. This is definitely not allowed for a monk, especially one so junior, but he felt confident in echoing the carefree spirit he saw in his master. After all, if the master was doing it, it must be okay.

Upon their return to the monastery Ajahn Chah, wise to these goings-on, stood before his errantly-robed disciple. Reaching out, and with a fierce look in his eye, he grabbed the akimbo garment and yanked it forcefully back to its proper position. Without a word he walked away.

Though wordless, his teaching couldn't be clearer: the master soars free on the wings of superior artistry; the fledgling must follow the rules to the letter until their own wings have taken form. Although, as a strategy, "fake it till you make it" can help to carve grooves that head in the right general direction, when it comes to mastery there is no faking it. Flap as we may, while our wings are still only mere stubs we won't get off the ground.

Poetic license

The unfettered improvisation of mastery brings to mind the idea of poetic license, where wordsmiths may deviate from the conventional usage of the tools of their trade—from the normal rules of spelling or grammar—in order to produce a result that grammatical orthodoxy would put out of reach. Unburdened by standard procedure, the freedom of poetic license allows the poet to craft a turn of phrase that renders as a living thing a slice of life that over-reliance on proper usage might pin to the corkboard as a dusty dead specimen.

Although, when viewed in isolation and out of context, such usage of words would surely be "wrong," when seen in their rightful place—as parts of an unfolding flow of artistry—no other rendering would do. This is the gift of the master: to reach beyond the limitations of an arbitrary blueprint of yesses and noes and to craft, using the prompts of an unfolding moment in time, a perfect expression of aptness. Of course, such a practice can only be fit when employed with a deep understanding of wordcraft, and sensitivity to what is needed right now. Without those, poetic license is just an excuse for putting words to bad use.

The master, then, whatever their genre, is at liberty to make use of poetic license in doing what it is that they do. Over-reliance on rules is cast off as a straitjacket and replaced by reliance on letting the influx of now shape our actions. Masters of music, of dance, of art, of living and life have always paid allegiance first to the needs of the moment as it arises, moving in harmony with it, flowing in love with it; only secondarily are the arbitrary rules of the art form observed as the theme song that underscores an already perfect performance.

A perilously fine line, though, divides the master who responds uninhibitedly to the moment from someone who thinks they can do as they please. The difference, at times hard to see on the outside, is loud in the heart of the doer. We cannot know the heart of another, but we can know our own. We know if we're simply bending the rules to suit our own dubious agenda or to justify shonky behaviour. Perhaps, too, we know if our actions are the effortless doings of nature making use of our gift of a well-prepared conduit.

Noble humility

The master is certainly one who is no longer slave to a host of demeaning restrictions. But that doesn't mean they fall into the nonsense of lordship or self-aggrandizement, for one who has mastered is one who has fully surrendered—to their art form, to its principles, to the flowing nature of now. No longer concerned with enforcement of will the master lets life unfold, but steered with a steady hand that won't go awry. Mastery sees the great hand of nature at work in all that is done, a hand that cannot fumble, and to see that is to know the sweetness and the potency of humility.

That humility has always been the hallmark of true masters; it is the badge of their authenticity. And that humility sees that the mastery of a thing has only ever been the mastery of oneself. And that mastery of oneself is not something other than putting oneself aside and allowing the blood of the cosmos to come rushing in and fill up the space.

Here it is no longer the "person" who acts, for that has been laid to one side. You could say it is nature manifesting itself through the master's performance. You could say it's the spirit of the art form coming to life. You could say the universe is finding expression through a well-prepared vessel of flesh and of mind and of heart, that it has a way now to shine through the deeds of the masterful one. After a lifetime of drawing the bow, master archer Awa Kenzo found a way to describe how it is:

> The Bow becomes oneself. To learn about the Bow
> is to learn about oneself. To learn about oneself is
> to forget the self. To forget self is to realize that all
> things in the universe are you. From the beginning,
> heaven and earth are you, from start to finish. We
> are all from the same source, one with the cosmos.[4]

To stand aside and allow the optimum course of events to unfold through a body-mind tuned to the tune of the moment, that is to be set adrift and yet anchored in mastery. When we feel keenly the air of the moment; when we eschew resistance to the way things are; when we leave uncommitted the thoughts, words and deeds that would scald our innards and coarsen our world; when we effortlessly compliment the good and redirect the malignant; when these things are first nature, done as our first response to the inflows of now, then the principles of divine laziness have taken root and are free to give forth the nourishing bounty of mastery.

And when we see that all this is happening as naturally as water running downhill, then we may see that all we have done is come home, where the heart is, and all we need do is stay here.

Chapter Eight

A Case of Divine Laziness:
Wing Chun as an Art of Living Effortlessly

To walk the way of divine laziness is a possibility wherever we may be; it can (and I say it should) form the basis of our approach to all of the varied activities of life. But certain contexts—like the training-grounds offered by various art forms—lend themselves particularly well to its cultivation, based as they are on a currency of sensitivity and effortlessness; while we are poor in this coin our efforts to flourish will buy very little. Training within such an environment gives unremitting feedback on how we are progressing, and lets us know with (sometimes painful) sharpness when we have abandoned sensitivity and effortlessness in favour of brute force or numb neglect. Missteps are seen much more clearly within the dance of that artistry than set against the more nebulous backdrop of life in general.

Many are the art forms that provide such fertile ground for cultivation, and any genuine one will no doubt demand of us a very high degree of sensitivity and effortlessness before any notions of mastery can be entertained. And any of them may also, when followed with an emphasis on using them to cultivate sensitivity and effortlessness, lead us straight to the heart of divine laziness.

This has been the case (at least for me) with the exploration of wing chun[1], which I offer here as a concrete example of how divine laziness may be "done" in our lives through the art forms we follow with love. When I listen to the heart of wing chun I hear it beat to the rhythm of divine laziness. It is purely my own experiences within this art form, and my own understanding of its principles and practices, that singles it out as a tributary to the tide of effortless living. Others approaching it may do so from a wholly different perspective and with another agenda entirely. With them I have no argument; I only hold wing chun up like this because it has played such a pivotal role in my own attempts at effortless living. It has shown to me how sensitivity and effortlessness can be practiced in tangible ways, how they are "done." It has shown me how abandoning these principles scuppers our attempts at artistry and renders us lame on our walk to freedom. Perhaps most of all it has shown me how important training is in building our sensitivity and heightening our effortlessness, and how, through practice, we can actually watch those things grow.

If we have no codified field of study in which we sculpt our behaviour and nurture our realization, it is to the raw material of our lives that we must turn as the training ground of our sensitivity and effortlessness—to our interpersonal doings, to the way we shape our interactions, to the finesse we bring or don't to each moment. This, in the end, is where our training must ultimately take place anyway, though it is that much more difficult for the absence of a steadfast teacher or ready scaffold of principles and rules to keep us in check when our tendencies pull us around.

The surrender of ourselves to an art form that takes us to the heart of our lives—one that makes us bow our head in reverence—is therefore an adjunct that greatly reduces the trial-and-error that must otherwise dog our footsteps on this, our greatest journey. And to find the fingerprints of divine laziness upon the face and pressed into the heart of that art form gives our training the utmost urgency while asking us to relax into the utmost ease.

Planting the seeds of kung fu

Kung fu has always made an eligible consort for the contemplative path to freedom (despite their seemingly mismatched attire when viewed from afar), their mythologies being intertwined in part through the legendary personage of Bodhidharma. Revered as the 28th patriarch of Zen, Bodhidharma was an Indian Buddhist monk who, upon traveling by sea to China in the 5th or 6th century, set about with the transmission there of Zen Buddhism[2]. He also, according to tradition, planted during his stay at the Shaolin temple seeds that would grow into the distinctly Chinese family of martial arts known collectively as kung fu.

Bodhidharma's extremely intense approach is one of his most defining and endearing characteristics; he famously sat gazing at a cave wall for nine years—long enough for the sun to burn an image of his silhouette into the rock face—before entering the nearby monastery where his teachings that would be the rudiments of kung fu took root. He also reputedly cut off his own eyelids in an attempt (successful, I imagine) to prevent sleepiness from hampering his meditation. And in the same vein of uncompromising toughness, a prospective disciple is said to have lopped off his own arm to demonstrate his sincerity and determination to be accepted as a student, so ardently did he desire to drink from the cup of Bodhidharma's wisdom. Or so the legends go.

But alongside that hard core of unrelenting rigor we find teachings that give voice to a profound peace and release from the slings and arrows of misery that blacken the skies of mortal life. We find verses that speak of the great ease of simply being, an ease that requires no going afar to discover.

> To find a buddha all you have to do is see your nature. Your nature is the buddha. And the buddha is the person who's free: free of plans, free of cares. If you don't see your nature and run around all day looking somewhere else, you'll never find a buddha. The truth is, there's nothing to find.[3]

> If you're not sure, don't act. Once you act, you wander through birth and death and regret not having a refuge. Poverty and hardship are created by false thinking. To understand this mind you have to act without acting.[4]

> A buddha is an idle person. He doesn't run around after fortune and fame. What good are such things in the end?[5]

This is the voice of radical non-doing from one who spared no efforts doing what it took to realize it. And the training halls of kung fu still ring (for those with ears to hear) with that voice, a roar from the chest of one who has come fully to rest. Such a roar fills the silence with a call to freedom: the freedom of non-doing won through to by extraordinary feats; the freedom of effortlessness arrived at through well-guided effort; the freedom to act without acting and to be what we are without doing. When viewed in this light kung fu does indeed wear the robe of divine laziness.

Divine laziness in action

There are many reasons for studying a martial art: to better understand oneself; to grow in confidence and finesse; to follow an art form to the heart of living. Some even do it to get good at fighting. I hope the foregoing chapters have made it obvious that my own motives for studying kung fu have nothing to do with violence; quite to the contrary, I consider it to be the art of dissolving any violence that spoils a person. And to that end I have found a powerful solvent in the branch of kung fu known as wing chun. That's not to say that wing chun isn't effective for fighting or self defense—it undoubtedly is, and exceptionally so—but that's not what makes it really interesting. That's not what makes it an art of effortless living.

What does is the way it so clearly and tangibly embodies the sensitivity and effortlessness that lie at the heart of divine laziness. Training in this art form offers a direct way to cultivate these, a definitive roadmap for planting the flag of divine laziness in the soil of one's life. The path of wing chun, if walked just so, is an avenue straight to the heart of it all. I think of it as divine laziness in action.

The nun at the dawn of wing chun

In symmetry with the origins of kung fu itself, and reinforcing the ties between the spirits of kung fu and Buddhist practice, the founding of wing chun is attributed to a Buddhist nun. Ng Mui was her name, one of the legendary Five Masters of kung fu who survived the destruction of the Shaolin Temple in China during the Qing dynasty. It is said that Ng Mui developed the theories upon which wing chun is based by observing the movements of various animals as they fought (a crane in combat with a fox or a snake being popular characters in the tale). Whether her tale is historical fact or a flight of fancy is not so important as the assertion that the system was developed by a woman, and a Buddhist nun at that, the epitome of softness and gentleness. In a genre that prizes might and power it is interesting indeed to claim such a delicate genesis.

What this origin story points to is a crucial premise that underlies the art: it is not strength that must be relied on, but lightness and sureness of touch. Thus a smaller, weaker person can overcome a larger, stronger attacker by using efficient techniques based on the natural mechanics of the human body cleverly harnessed. This way necessarily forgoes the use of force against force, otherwise the weaker one surely would fail in a battle of brawn. How many rounds would a Buddhist nun go against bullies and bandits with only her strength to rely on? Instead, in wing chun force is withheld and the structure of well-honed techniques is relied upon to receive and redirect the brunt of an attack. And as we control that incoming force we set it to work in our favour, and against its expender; the harder they push, the further they push themselves into a corner. And then, only then, when the time is just right, we may add a little strength of our own, just enough to knock the last nail into the coffin that our strong-armed opponent has hammered together unwittingly.

A similar strategy could be employed by an engineer charged with the task of manipulating massive blocks of stone. The skillful application of leverage achieves with only minuscule effort on his part what would be impossible were he to forgo his lever and pulley and instead throw himself into the task with nothing but muscle. The lever and pulley are our wing chun techniques; by aligning with principles of physics they deliver the power of nature itself without wasting a drop of their own finite potency. This is the idea of minimum effort rightly applied for maximum result. This is the principle of effortlessness in action.

Wing chun excels in this vein as the art and science of using the human biomechanical structure efficiently. Within the context of martial application this means using the least amount of effort necessary to overcome an opponent, regardless of their relative stature and power. But deeper than that, wing chun teaches us to finely feel, through our contact with the world around us, the subtle nuances of each and every now, and to respond with just the right energy, in just the right way, and to do so without forcing or fighting.

The yin principle

The tale of the womanly inception of wing chun invites us to follow in those founding footsteps by "acting like a woman;" that is, we are asked to bring forth qualities that may be thought of as feminine. In this light is it perhaps more useful to think of the art being founded *on* the feminine principle rather than *by* a woman.

The feminine principle (yin in Taoist philosophy) has the attributes of softness, receptivity, contraction, silence, relaxation and passivity, as contrasted with the masculine principle (yang) which embodies hardness, penetration, expansion, noise, tension, activity. This in no way implies that the feminine principle applies only to women and the masculine to men. Gender is another matter entirely, and each embodies both yin and yang qualities. Rather, these are universal principles that can be observed all around, their combination in all things making up their hardness or softness, their lightness or darkness, their silence or thunderous clamor.

These contrasting and complimentary principles have occupied for eons a place at the heart of Chinese mystical thought and fund the characteristically inclusive stance found there. And, though both are equally essential, in many respects it is the feminine principle that has been revered as the most profitable course to follow. From the Tao Te Ching:

> The female surmounts the male by her stillness.[6]

> The softest vanquishes the hardest.
> That which is empty of substance can find a way in,
> even where there are no openings.
> Therefore I recommend non-doing.[7]

The soft has been praised all along as the way of overcoming the hard, like the formless waves of the ocean that gradually wear down the hardest of rocks and reduce them to nothing but sand. Thus wing chun's efficacy springs from its roots in the feminine principle: offering no resistance, the gentlest may vanquish the hardest of things; having no substance we find a way in even where there seems to be no space.

Were we to proceed using masculine attributes alone, such as strength and force, then the biggest and strongest would win and it would be pointless for the weaker ones to bother getting started in the first place. Legions of other forms take up this stance; these have little to offer the wayfarer on the path of divine laziness. But for we of wing chun it is the principle of yin that primarily guides our kung fu, and once our techniques have been developed to an adequate degree our primary concern is to remain relaxed and composed, sensitive to the movements and energies coming our way. Only right at the end, once our tactics of yin have brought us right up to the goal do we unleash the yang to finish the job; by then it is too late to fail.

Sticky hands

Few art forms are as well equipped as wing chun when it comes to ascending the threefold developmental process examined in chapter three. This is mainly due to its training methods being based around physical interaction with another person. Once the basic techniques have been learned they are trained more and more in response to input from another practitioner.

This interpersonality gives us a highly tangible arena for honing sensitivity—we must feel acutely what our training partner is up to if we are to respond in a suitable way—as well as immediate feedback on our own energy output, whether too great or too small. It also provides effective motivation to apply that sensitivity and effortlessness well, and to continually develop our skill: any lapse on our part and we will be hit. (We're not really trying to hit each other, by the way; we train in a spirit of co-operation and mutual advancement. Even so, if our techniques are shoddy or our perimeter lax, our partner will easily exploit those weaknesses and we will "lose"). The threat of being "hit" keeps us focused intensely on our movements and, as we have seen, sensitivity to present happenings lets us respond with effortlessness.

As touched on in chapter three, one of the principle training tools in the wing chun system is an exercise known as chi sau, or "sticky hands," named so for the way that our hands "stick" to our partner's, establishing and maintaining a connection with them at all times. This sticking provides a constant readout of tactile data that informs us of our partner's position, their movements, and—when we become sensitive enough—their intentions.

Chi sau is not sparring and has little to do with fighting. It is simply a way for two practitioners to help one another hone their skills. Those skills have four facets, all of which chi sau develops: 1) techniques, 2) energy, 3) angles, 4) sensitivity. Of these four the last—sensitivity—is the most important; without adequate sensitivity and the fitting response it enables the other three will fall flat. Unless we can feel the position of our partner and how they are moving, our techniques will not be in tune with them; our energy cannot be evoked and adjusted in relation to them; the angles we use in positioning our techniques have nothing to go on. But when led by the hand of sensitivity these instruments are made subtle and sharp.

The chi sau conversation

The chi sau exchange can be thought of as being like a conversation. Two people skilled at conversing, with ears to hear and with interests aligned and a well-known vocabulary at their disposal, may speak into being a thing of great beauty and worth. By listening with care they pick up the subtlest cues that inform how they phrase their response. But those with ears stopped up are deaf to all but the loudest and coarsest of calls. With a mouthful of anesthetic and a stunted vocabulary we can only mutter and grunt in response, or shout incoherent replies.

So it is with the tools employed in the workings of chi sau as well: our ears that comprise the defensive perimeter hear what our partner is saying, and how loud, and with what kind of temper, and perceive their intent; our techniques are the mouthpiece that speaks our response, plucked from a vocabulary of tactics rooted in yesterday's training.

Until we've grown sensitive and learned to receive we just shout at each other with rigid and forceful techniques. Bellowing back and forth like a couple of drunkards is hardly a conversation. But once we soften and develop in sensitivity we can become attuned to even a whisper from our partner, a whisper that may speak volumes about their intentions. Our responses too can be as refined.

Such an exchange is made possible only when both people listen intently to each others movements. The sharper our hearing the finer the things we can hear and the more apt our answer will be, provided we possess the dialect with which to express it. As our sensitivity grows so too does our eloquence. And should the conversation become a debate, one who can listen profoundly (and therefore reply to the point) will always win out over one who can not. Like in any conversation, like in any exchange, skill in wing chun lies in learning to listen.

Give up your strength

Crucial to sensitivity is our ability to relax; stiffness and hardness feel nothing. The relaxation needed is not just a lack of energy; such slackness collapses our defensive perimeter and robs our techniques of their footing. Rather, what is required is use of the right energy at the right time. We use only enough energy to achieve our aim, and only when the moment is ripe. And when we apply that energy we do so in tune with the way the situation is moving. Non-resistant, we deliver our actions with effortlessness. How that is actually done is spelled out in four maxims:

1. Relinquish your strength.

First we relax. While we meet our partner with resistance we ruin any chance of feeling the cues that tell us how to respond to them. This non-resistance is the crux of chi sau, and until it is learned we are merely engaged in a battle of strength.

Forgoing the use of force against force our response to encroachment is likened to water: as liquid it offers no resistance but yields to receive whatever we care to throw at it, without giving up its integrity. But when water turns into ice, rigid and strong, its glacial structure won't yield and can only resist; if struck by a strong enough blow it will shatter. Our defensive perimeter acts in a similar way; while malleable like liquid it greets and absorbs each intrusion; should we stiffen up, rigid like ice, our defense will be dashed by a force sufficiently strong. Again from Lao Tsu:

> At birth we are supple and soft; when we die we are rigid and stiff.
>
> Saplings are tender and supple. Trees when they die are brittle and dry.
>
> Therefore the hard and strong follow the path of death, while the gentle and soft walk the way of life.
>
> Those who stick to strategies or brandish their might can never triumph.
>
> The hard and strong sink to the bottom.
>
> The gentle and soft rise to the top.[10]

Worse still for the hard and the strong, too much strength in our techniques can be used against us by a sufficiently skilled opponent, the effort we throw into the exchange thrown right back at us. We only end up bullying ourselves.

2. Redirect your opponent's strength.

When incoming force is received we neither resist nor collapse, but use our defensive perimeter to redirect it. That defensive perimeter—which incorporates all parts of the body into a structure that is resilient, responsive and able to change in an instant—meets and receives an advancement from our opponent. Then, rather than opposing, it redirects that force to where it will work in our favour and against its owner.

It works like this: imagine we are standing face to face with someone, both arms outstretched palm-to-palm with those of the other person. Now imagine we both start pushing against one another, and the game is to try to push the other person over. Eventually whoever is stronger will win, through sheer muscle might, and that's no game at all (especially if we're not the stronger one). But if instead we suddenly step to one side and remove our opposing force from the mix, our cohort will topple forward by their own exertion while we stand aside out of harm's way. They have, in effect, pushed themselves over.

This is the strategy of redirection. Non-resistant, we receive and redirect without opposing. An uncontrolled use of redirection like that in the example above gets us out of the way well enough but does not maintain control of the energy redirected, so cannot detain or repurpose it. Ideally, though, our movement would place us in a position that increases our advantage while robbing the attacker of their stability. And, by keeping a handle on the diverted energy, we may use it for our own purposes.

To do this we need sensitivity to determine the moment at which we should yield, through feeling precisely how much effort is being exerted by our opponent, and how much force our perimeter can handle without being compromised. And we need to determine the way we must move to compliment the momentum of their energy without jumping into the firing line.

3. Borrow your opponent's strength.

Once successfully redirected, the opponent's incoming force can be harnessed to drive our response. This is reminiscent of old style jousting dummies used for training by knights on horseback. Mounted atop a post on a pivot that enabled it to swivel through a full rotation of 360 degrees, the dummy had two arms protruding from its torso; upon one was mounted a shield and to the other was fastened a swinging sack or weapon of some kind. The knight would ride toward the dummy with his lance leveled at the shield arm. The impact caused the dummy to swivel around on the post; the weapon mounted to its other arm would provide, as it swung, an "attack" for the knight to avoid, thereby enhancing his training. The dummy, like the wing chun practitioner, would borrow the force from the blow of the lance and use it to launch its own counter-attack.

To act like that dummy requires, of course, that we move. Standing stiff and unyielding before an onslaught is asking for bruises. We take ourselves out of harm's way by yielding and redirecting the incoming force. And, once redirected, that force becomes ours to employ as we will, provided we're in a position to use it.

4. Add your own strength.

Only once the previous three conditions are in place—having relaxed we successfully redirect an incoming force, commandeering any strength given over in the process—do we apply this final component and bring forth our own store of energy to "finish the job" as it were. But even then any force we deliver is complimentary to the conditions at hand, not at odds with them; if they are moving away we follow; if they are coming towards we detain; if they are moving in we turn to one side and shut down their charge with the angle thus newly established. Even when delivering our own energy, still we observe non-resistance.

Taken together this quartet of maxims—relinquish your strength; redirect their strength; borrow their strength; add your own strength—represents the practical application of effortlessness. When coupled with the sensitivity that effortlessness depends upon—sensitivity to the ebb and flow of our partner; to the substance and shape of our stance and techniques, and the whispers that guide our responses—what we have is a complete training ground for the development of divine laziness. What we have is a laboratory fully equipped to grow the enlazening process. What we have is a studio ripe for crafting the art of living effortlessly. With such a full suite of facilities at one's disposal the chance of a masterpiece happening may not be so bad.

In the meantime we can visit some of the principles that underpin wing chun. There are a number of them, but two stand out as uppermost for consideration here: centerline, and economy of movement.

Centerline

Wing chun is built around the centerline. It is the linchpin that fastens the entire system. This line emanating forward from the center of our body is the zone we endeavour to protect, containing as it does our most vulnerable areas. It is also the plane that the wing chun practitioner seeks to control in the deployment of their art.

The first form learned by a student of wing chun is called siu nim tau, which means "little idea." There are no grand movements or flamboyance to be seen, just the slow and steady development of the basic techniques that make up the system. And a meticulous cultivation of familiarity with the centerline. Our feet don't move at all in siu nim tau—a stable and static stance is developed instead —but our hand techniques are trained to know the centerline so well that we feel it like a limb.

If they are to be effective our focus and techniques must occupy the centerline. Straying to one side or the other gives away our control of it. Without that control we cannot hope to maintain our defense, much less manipulate that of another person. Also, because the stability of our structure is built around its relationship with the centerline, techniques that fall too far to one side will not work. In fact, they will probably work against us. We must inhabit the space between left and right.

So often our focus does fall to one side or the other, our techniques too far left or right, our aim not quite true. But through practice we learn to feel this deviation (usually just before we get hit) and over time we begin to know it as the harbinger of our downfall. We feel when we vacate the centerline and know that we're asking for trouble.

Life has a centerline too

Our movement through life can likewise adhere to or diverge from a centerline, one defined by the principles of effortless living. When our aim is true and our actions fall neither too far to one side or the other we rest in the ease of knowing that we are safeguarded. But if we flail about wildly with the limbs of our doing we discard our composure and open ourselves up to a clobbering. A well-trained feel for the centerline keeps us on track, or at least helps us know where the track is when we wander off piste and end up in a ditch.

The notion of the centerline also echoes a core theme of Buddhist philosophy and practice: the middle way. This is the gateway between extremes; the extremes of holding on and pushing away, of fanaticism and slackness; the extremes of too little and too much, of all or nothing. We can navigate extremes without falling into either by simply walking between them. Beholding and understanding this middle way is said to have been the straw that broke the back of delusion and led to the Buddha's awakening.

The catalyst for that awakening was hearing the instructions of a passing master musician to his student: the sitar string too tightly wound will snap; too loose and it won't sound; it must be tuned just so. This advice for tuning sitars also held good, realized the buddha-to-be, for walking the path to freedom and so he adjusted his bearing accordingly. Having arrived at the brink of death through fruitless ascetic practices, the adoption of this more moderate stance led to a cascade of insights that demolished delusion completely. By avoiding extremes he discovered the middle way leading to understanding. The same prescription has guided the multitudes who have followed him since.

We too can avoid the extremes of one side or the other and maintain focus on the narrow, infallible avenue that falls into neither. By learning to feel then learning to keep to the centerline we set ourselves up to always be right where we need to be, and to sense the danger inherent in deviation.

Economy of movement

There is a wing chun saying: "Others walk the bow, I walk the string." The shortest distance between two points is a straight line, and the circuitous route of walking the curve of the bow will always take longer than walking the straight line of the string. Loath to do more than we need to, our techniques move in a straight line rather than circularly. One advantage of hands that inhabit the centerline is they are already where they need to be when the time comes for them to move in attack or defense. This is how one skilled at wing chun appears to be so fast, always seeming to get to the target before it even knows it's a target. It's not that their movements are especially speedy, they just don't travel further than they need to. They walk the string and make their opponent walk the bow, and so embody a technical speed rather than that of velocity.

In wing chun we don't do more than required. If we do and we're up against one who is sensitive we're sunk. This I have learned only too well. Time and again I overdo it; I throw in too much energy and those with enough sensitivity and skill use that energy to engineer my downfall. This is the way it works in chi sau, and this is the way it works in our lives. But when all of our strategies of brute force have been exhausted we are left with no other option but taking up residence in the right kind of laziness. That laziness doesn't waste a single joule of effort on what is not needed.

Back in the Seventies Bruce Lee made popular one of the classic utensils of wing chun training: the one-inch-punch. Executed with the hand only a short distance away from its target (usually more than an inch to be honest, but the name is cool nevertheless), the one-inch-punch is a simple extension of the arm that belies the power it delivers. It is used to demonstrate, to oneself and and to onlookers, the power that can be generated from a very short range when the body works as a well-integrated unit. What could be more economic than a punch that barely travels at all? With so little movement involved all parts of the body must be justly aligned if the strike is to have any power. The whole body then delivers the punch by barely moving a muscle. It's not quantity but quality that determines a movement's effectiveness. With harmony even the slightest of acts can do much.

My sifu is fond of illustrating the thrifty use of movement by way of his "small door" theory. When we open a gap in our partner's defense that gap need only be wide enough to sneak our attacking hand through. We open a small door, no bigger than needed. A mere crack may suffice if we're subtle. Why go to the effort of pushing a door as far as its hinges will swing if there's only a waif coming through? And why would we open a gate the size of the side of a house if we're just going through on a bicycle? We're better off using a more modest opening, one that is fit for its purpose. But even when opening that adequate door, we do so without trying to force it, without opposing what's happening. (After all, we open a door according to how it's designed to be swung, not by trying to pound it into its frame.)

Three Cantonese maxims adorn the wall of my sifu's training hall, maxims that contain the essence of practice. Of these the one that is most often pointed to is roughly translated as this: "Receive what comes, follow what goes."[11] If they want to come in we bring them to us; if they are retreating we follow. We compliment the way the movement is already going by adding "more of the same," and in this way much of our work is done for us. Not only do we not resist what is happening, by helping it along with a little nudge of our own we manage far more than what would be possible by force. The way we might, for example, keep a heavy revolving door spinning with the merest touch of a finger, a touch that would never get it moving from stationary.

One further key to economy of motion is accomplishing several objectives with a single action. In wing chun there is the concept of simultaneous attack and defense; both are delivered together, two jobs done at the same time. We do away with the need to take two "beats" to accomplish first a defense and then a counter-attack; both spring to life on the same beat. "One count, not two," as my sifu often says; both land at once. Moreover, as well as not wasting beats by having to complete a defense before we can mobilize any counter-attack, we can also be thrifty with limbs by delivering both the defense and attack with the same one; a single technique to do both. Our defensive hand is also the striking hand. Our step that evades an onslaught is also the footwork that encroaches upon the encroacher. We kill two birds with one stone, so to speak (or feed two dogs with one bone, to use an image more palatable to we who happen to like our avian friends).

Where others may spend an entire limb on blocking a strike, then fritter away an additional limb on delivering a strike of their own, our single action stops their attack while completing our own. Two birds, one stone. Doing no more than is needed, accomplishing several tasks with a single action, marks us as fine contenders for the prize of the laziest.

These two principles, centerline and economy of movement, infuse and imply one another. We can keep our movements to a minimum yet achieve great effectiveness when we stay on the centerline. And being already in place on that centerline we have but a short way to move when we need to. And what a fine model for life: if we stay in the optimum place we don't need to struggle to get where we need to be to do what we need to do. We're already here.

Sut duk geem sau

To train as the bearer of martial prowess alone without reference to a code of decency is a dangerous road that can lead into thuggery. If we are to aim ourselves at the heart of such an art form we would do well to also adhere to a moral code that ensures our aim stays true. Far from being at odds, these two—the development of skills that are martial in nature and the brightening of one's moral rectitude—embrace one another, adding a mutual sheen.

My training in wing chun has unfolded beneath the motto of my sifu's school, "Sut duk geem sau," which translates as "cultivating martial skill and moral uprightness together." The development of one's moral character is the prerequisite as well as the product of building the skills that make up kung fu. Chief among these abilities is the capacity of the heart to retain its composure in the thick of adversity. And as that capacity is developed, the heart so composed finds itself getting closer to others, not further away. A true martial art is no more about beatings than the art of archery is about shooting people; of course one who has developed such skills can use them to that end, but the very training that acquires them tends to rub the hatred out too. Those who are in it to fight are still only scratching the surface.

But to those who find the true heart of a martial art nothing could be plainer: that heart is the home of compassion and it glows with a warmth that seeks to nurture the world, not to scorch it. Master Morihei Ueshiba founded the art of Aikido on this understanding:

> The Art of Peace does not rely on weapons or brute force to succeed; instead we put ourselves in tune with the universe, maintain peace in our own realms, nurture life, and prevent death and destruction. The true meaning of the term samurai is one who serves and adheres to the power of love.[12]

Those who see this from the inside are not concerned with mere battlefield tactics, nor with the swelling of brutality. The world is sick enough with the violence and one-upmanship that has us at each others throats. Our hearts are harrowed enough by the hatred and belligerence that feed the nightmare of hostility. Our path is one that seeks to extinguish those blistering embers and ignites instead the flame of brotherhood and peace.

My sifu often says that it's not enough to learn wing chun, you've got to practice it. And it's not enough to practice wing chun, you've go to live it. The same is true for any form of art we would follow to the heart of this life. Its principles and practices are not to be left in the training hall, forgotten as we go through the rest of our lives, but must form and inform the substratum of how we engage in everything we do. And if its principles and practices put us in tune with the universe, if its manner of training maintains peace and prevents destruction and discord, then we are treading a path that leads the right way. With sensitivity and effortlessness as its marrow and its methods wing chun is indeed such a path.

Chapter Nine

Already Free

SO FAR WE'VE BEEN proceeding on the assumption that we are somehow separate from everything else, that we are "in here" and the rest is "out there." And the stuff out there pushes and pummels (and maybe if we're lucky it kisses and comforts) the one in here, and the one in here does what it can to manage, for better or worse, that stuff out there, and never shall they meet.

This "one in here" that we tend to identify with so fiercely—the constellation of things that are clumped together and then labeled "me"—is only a story. It is the story of our life. It tells of this body, this mind, these thoughts and these actions; it tells of the things that we do and do not, have done and have not, shall do and shan't. All that we want and all we avoid, all we attend to and all we neglect, and everything that we assume; these are the plot and the players that render this phantasm so believable. And they do a fine job, but it's still just a story.

The entire contents of that story comes and it goes. Each chapter starts and it ends. We watch it all as it flares into being then withers and dies or goes out with a bang. The very fact that we see it all dissolve makes it obvious that none of it qualifies as being what we are. And the fact that each and every word of that story takes shape and dissolves in response to other things shows that none of it is innately actual; none of it, in that sense, is real.

Yet there is the conviction that we are somehow utterly at stake in all of this, and that it is therefore terribly important that we do the right things and avoid doing the wrong things; that we have the right kinds of experiences and avoid the wrong ones; that we earn the tick of approval from those around us and from ourselves, and escape the black stain of deficiency. All of our doings are directed by this and all of our struggles are marked by the drive to get it right and not get it wrong.

Do this and don't do that

We come up with strategies to make of our lives a landscape we wish to inhabit, a landscape free form the brambles of misery and difficulty, one pleasing to walk through and rich in the bounty of goodness. Principles and practices picked up and nurtured by us are employed to that end, be they consciously chosen endeavors like the suggestions contained in this book, or social injunctions that hack off our yearnings or stuff us with gumption and fling us into the fray.

We identify schemes and behaviours that tend to mire us in that which is undesirable, and advise one another to avoid them. And we seek out those strategies that tend towards freedom and ease, towards that which we want and away from what we despise, and encourage each other to pursue them. And all these suggestions boil down to one basic directive: do this and don't do that.

When we embark on a path we believe will take us to freedom and ease we do so by fixing our lives to a scaffold of do-this-and-don't-do-that. Any true path is replete with such biddings and, as we've explored in the foregoing pages, these are the means by which we may make of our lives a story worth living. These are the lifelines that save us from drowning. On such a path, consciously followed, every do-this and each don't-do-that is a signpost to wisdom, a pointer to freedom. Following the road they mark out bends our lives to the shape of the heart: sensitive, free from pushing or pulling, deeply aware and at ease.

But follow such paths as we may, the truth is it makes not a smidgen of difference to that which *knows* the comings and goings of all of the doings that seek to arrange our lives to be this and not that. All this activity is merely a storm in a teacup. And like any good storm being watched through a window, though it exhilarates some and may terrify others, it's harmless to the watcher who stays cozy and dry on this side of the glass. Perhaps it's our own reflection we see in the window that makes us believe there's some poor soul out there getting drenched. But no matter how dramatic the storm is, none of it can have anything to do with who—or what —we really are, for surely if there is anything that deserves being claimed as an "I" it is that which remains while all of that turbulence comes rolling in and then blows itself out. Sifting among the windswept debris, see if there's anything lasting.

The knowing

What is it that is always here? Amidst all of the coming and going, what stays? What is the same today as it was last year and last night as we slept, when we were five years old and before we were born? What common factor has been here all along? None of the things that have come and gone in the meantime qualify—none of the thoughts or feelings, none of the happiness or horror, not our great achievements nor our spectacular failures, and none of the nondescript moments between. Yet each and every microsecond of that has been known.

Ever present is the knowing of whatever arises. In fact, to say a thing has arisen is to say it has been known: it has arisen to knowing. There's no happening other than what is known, and each thing that happens is known as it happens with consummate clarity. Even the protest that we don't know a thing or that we only dimly perceive it, is known as it is, perfectly clearly.

It's not intellectual knowing we're looking for here, that of a "me" that is pointing its conscious attention at some particular target picked out against everything else. That is just conscious attention, another activity. And that's known as it's happening too. We're looking for the knowing that's going on anyway, unstoppably, causelessly, totally naturally, prior to thought and before any deliberation. Poets and priests and saints and sinners have groped through the ages for ways of describing this. We can just call it the knowing.

The knowing is all that persists in a world of constant dissolution. Nothing can be done to prevent the knowing from knowing, and nothing we do can fall outside of its ken. Any state at all, whether shining clarity or dingy obscurity, laser-like focus or deep catatonia, is known as it happens, just as it is, with utter and unstinting clarity. Whether we're soaring the heights of lucidity or have fallen down drunk in a ditch, the knowing knows all of it. <u>All</u> of it.

Try it and see. Look right now; is it not true that everything that is arising is known as it does so? Doesn't this happen whether we mean it to happen or not, that in fact the entirety of body and mind—of all we call "me"—is known immediately as it comes into existence, moment after moment after commonplace moment?

Was there ever a moment that came into being without being known? Is there anything happening outside of this knowing? Must we spend our lives searching for something more special than this; a sharper vision, a clearer perceiving, a mystical something other than ordinary everyday this? Is there some other reality we need to uncover in order to be happy and free?

Forget some special secret reality elsewhere. This *is* that special secret reality. And it's as plain as can be.

Moreover, the knowing receives it all, and accepts it all, and embraces it all, and loves it all. Its arms are held wide for the sweet things, for sure, but even the wretched little horrors that can seem to make up so much of our lives are contained in the knowing's loving embrace. For real love has no notion of judgment or rejection; it always and only welcomes it all just because it exists. And the knowing is that love. And we are that knowing.

Perhaps we imagine some entity that exists among the myriad pieces of flotsam and jetsam that litter the shores of experience, an entity to look at and point at and cast as the knowing. But the knowing knows that looking as well: it knows as that notion of looking takes shape; it knows as that looking arises; it knows as that looking finds what it seeks, or the drama devised as it fails. The knowing is not to be seen in the seen; it's seeing that seeing as well. And there's nothing special about it. It's as plain as can be, even plainer; more ordinary than can be imagined. It's closer than close, more simple than simple, so obvious we just do not notice it. Until we do.

The Buddha's (very) first teaching

An age ago in an ancient land a man sat down at the foot of a tree and vowed he'd not rise again until he'd found the answer to the conundrum of human suffering. When he did get up it was as the Buddha—a title that means "the one who knows"—and he set out to share with humanity what he'd discovered. Taking to the road he made for the abode of a group of his former companions in the Quest. These would become his first students when he laid out before them the teaching that is known to history as setting in motion the rolling wheel of Dhamma.[1] But although that was his first formalized teaching, it was not the first thing he shared with another human after his seated odyssey beneath the bodhi tree.

On the road from the foot of that tree to set that wheel rolling he was met by a wayfarer who, impressed by his radiant countenance, asked who his teacher was, to which the Buddha replied:

> All-vanquishing, all-knowing am I.
> Untainted by all things.
> Abandoning all,
> with desire extinguished,
> I am released.
>
> This being perceived by myself, who can I point to?
> For me no teacher exists, and one like me cannot
> be found.
> In this world or the world of the gods
> There is no equal.
>
> For I am liberated in this world.
> I am the supreme master.
> I alone thoroughly and perfectly understand.
> I am calm and at peace.
>
> To set rolling the wheel of Dhamma
> I go to the town of Kasi
> For this blind world,
> To beat the drum of the deathless.[2]

As it turns out this assertion was somewhat too rich for its audience of one who simply responded with "May it be so" and, shaking his head, left by a different road.

This episode has mostly been written off by history as a slightly embarrassing failed first attempt at teaching by one who would later be hailed as a teacher beyond compare. And while the

Buddha went on to lay down a path leading back to his realization —a path rich in "do this and don't do that," well signposted and laid with precision and care—we can explore this first utterance as the naked report of what had been realized. (And here we may well be reminded of another famous statement of similar immediacy and intimacy, "I am the way, the truth and the life; no one comes to the Father but through me[3]," so evocative of a path leading inward.) This was no megalomaniac claiming some sort of personal mastery of heaven and earth. The Buddha was simply telling it how it is, giving voice to the knowing itself.

"All-vanquishing, all-knowing am I. Untainted by all things." What better description of that which is already free, and always and already knows what is happening as it is happening? Untouched by any of it, unmoved by all of it, ever pristine and unchanging.

"Abandoning all, with desire extinguished, I am released." That which is simply knowing has no need for hankering, and dwells not in any particular where. It simply sees all of it come and lets it all go. Such an I am is indeed released, for nothing can grasp it and ever has it been so.

"This being perceived by myself, who can I point to? For me no teacher exists, and one like me cannot be found. In this world or the world of the gods there is no equal." All the worlds of gods and men are made by the mind. They are born and they grow and they die right here within the knowing. Just as a potter won't find another potter among his various clay creations, so too do we find among the things of the world none equal to the knowing that knows them.

"For I am liberated in this world. I am the supreme master. I alone thoroughly and perfectly understand. I am calm and at peace." What we are is free of the world that arises within us, for none of it can besmirch the clear space of knowing that houses it, like the sky undisturbed by the beating wings of the bird that flies through it. That knowing within which all arises is thus the master of that all, and thoroughly and perfectly understands it all as it happens. This is a calmness that cannot be cracked; this is peace that cannot be shaken; neither are ever not present.

In a world that is blind, that which would make itself known must employ a medium other than sight to declare itself, and so is beaten the drum that counts out the rhythm of the deathless to a world that only dies. And if we can claim to be anything at all it is that which is deathless; all else disintegrates even as we behold it. The beat of the drum of the deathless is therefore none other than the pulse of oneself as the heart of all that there is.

Countless words have been spoken and written describing the ways we should be and the things we must do in order to get to the place that the Buddha called deathless. But surely that with no end has also no start and is already here. And being already here, how can our traveling in any direction bring us towards it or take us away? Instead of setting our sights on some distant horizon or something yet to be born, let us instead turn our attention to that which is already here and has always been here and has neither arrived nor departed.

Nothing new

The deathless knowing that we may then behold is of course nothing new, nothing special, nothing out of the ordinary. Actually it's the most ordinary aspect of now that there is. It's been here all along, far too obvious to notice, far too intimate to feel, far too simple to understand. It is what we are. "Self-realization is not acquisition of anything new nor is it a new faculty. It is only removal of all camouflage." These are the words of a sage who fell silent for years after waking spontaneously to reality at the age of sixteen; a silence that reigned perhaps because, for a time, all that was there was uncamouflaged knowing.[4]

That camouflage we build for ourselves. We dream this world into being then stuff it with beauty and horror, and then we believe we are that. But though it may be convincing and worn for so long our original face is forgotten, that camouflage does not and cannot alter our nature. A cat being dressed as a dragon does not make it a dragon. And so it is with the knowing, which can never be trapped in an ill-fitting sham and squashed by its weight and squeezed by its corsetry. The undisguised knowing that is what we are is already free.

Already free

Freedom is not to be found in some future or past or elsewhere, but right here now. Freedom is already totally present and fully formed and it is what we are. We have always been free of the lot of it, free of the pleasures as well as all the lament that has darkened the light of our lives. Suffering comes and goes before us and we remain unaffected.

A life free of suffering is not a life in which suffering does not arise—it does so in all of its miserable glory as torment of body and mind—but as it waxes and wanes we know we are free from its grip. It does not touch what we actually are, cannot harm us, cannot change us at all and never has, the way a storm leaves unmolested the sky that plays host to its raging tempestuousness.

Perhaps we may see that the world "out there" is nothing other than experiences known in here. They come and go within us. The sound of the wind or the bird in the tree are experiences that happen right here. There need not be any bird, any tree, any wind that exists somewhere else. They are right here within us; what we are includes all of that. There is no outside.

We find that we are not any of the particular things that make up the contents of the world because we are *all* of it. We see that anything happening in the realm of experience is not outside of us. It is happening right here. There is only right here. Where else could possibly exist? Even "over there" is arising right here. And all of it is happening without any special effort from us. This primal no-effort is our native state, where nothing is done at all, and yet everything comes and goes as it should. "Everything comes out of nothing and I watch as it all goes back there."[5]

And none of it matters. None of it. Not really. Even if we fall flat on our face to crawl in the dust of depravity, nothing can alter the immutable fact of our absolute freedom and intrinsic purity. There is absolutely nothing to do and nowhere to go. We are already here.

And yet...

But let us not make the mistake of assuming we may do as we please. Yes, we are free and there's nothing to do. And yet we must do this and avoid doing that. Even though we are free of this world that we sing to ourselves, still we must make it a song that gladdens the ear and quickens the heart and rises and falls in tune with the music of nature itself. Still we must smooth any dissonance that makes us a stranger to harmony.

The task our life charges us with is to bring its doings into alignment with that which breeds ease and ends conflict. Even though none of it matters to that which remains eternally free, nevertheless our activities must be aligned with what we actually are. Then our lives are an honest portrayal of the loving and ungrasping knowing that lies at the heart of it all.

Our life is the practice of freedom even though we are freedom itself and nothing can change that. Thus it is said: "Zen practice is the direct expression of our true nature."[6] The zen practice spoken of here is simply sitting and watching, our body and mind behaving as our true nature—the knowing—does; staying right here, relaxed and receptive and unperturbed as the world rises and falls. But the practice is also the effort to shed the superfluous, and the effortlessness of living a life that does not repel how it is.

Structuring our lives in this way can evoke several features: one is a growing clarity concerning our real nature; another is a background of happiness and ease, because we are no longer struggling to be at odds with ourselves. But if we insist on painting our lives in colours that clash with our actual hue we should not be surprised when those features are lost in the kaleidoscope. To live devoutly believing in that colourful show is to trap ourselves in a cage made out of the story, even though we are free and can never be trapped.

And there is the paradox.

We are perfectly unaffected by any of the comings and goings and doings of body and mind, and yet we must manifest that which is freeing (even though we are always and already free) and expunge that which enslaves us (even though it is no more possible to enslave that which is freedom itself than it is to catch sunbeams in a sack). And perhaps paradox is the only thing that rings true, so far as there can be any truth to the ring of a thing.

To not know the truth of what we are is to live as the miserable and dreary details of the story, and forever to grovel among them. To realize the truth, though, is happiness itself, and surely the goal of our lives. And that realization is within reach. And there are paths by which to reach it. And the art of living effortlessly may be such a path.

Yes we are pristine and beyond any stain. And yet we must bring forth the light that burns off the shadows that darken our innermost face.

Yes we are blameless, more innocent than newborns. And yet we must take up the task of clearing our name.

Yes we are already free and beyond all restriction. And yet we must follow the path that uncouples the chains that enslave us.

And if we should follow that path to the end we may see that we've never been anywhere and never done anything at all except everything that had to be done to arrive where we never departed from.

Notes

Chapter One

1. There are, of course, many genuine teachers of these arts whose offerings stand quite apart from the anemic versions appropriated by the mainstream.

2. In fact, the whole of the Buddhist path can be seen as the practice of uncovering and eradicating these roots, thereby eliminating misery at its source.

3. Lao Tsu, Tao Te Ching, ch. 48. Quotes from the Tao Te Ching that appear throughout this book are my own renderings, based on a number of the many English translations that have been made available over the last century or so. I make no claim to scholarly or literal accuracy; it is the gist or spirit of each chapter (as I see it) that I have tried to capture with these renderings.

Chapter Two

1. Lao Tsu, Tao Te Ching, ch. 37.

2. Ibid, chapter 1

3. A Dhammapada for contemplation, Ajahn Munindo (Verse 21)

4. "Ogha-tarana Sutta: Crossing over the Flood" (SN 1.1), translated from the Pali by Thanissaro Bhikkhu. Access to Insight (Legacy Edition), 30 November 2013, http://www.accesstoinsight.org/tipitaka/sn/sn01/sn01.001.than.html.

5. Morihei Uyeshiba, The Art of Peace by John Stevens, Shambhala Publications 2002

6. *Kamma* in Pali, the language of early Buddhism

7. A Dhammapada for contemplation, Ajahn Munindo. Verse 127

8. The Rubaiyat of Omar Khayyam (FitzGerald translation, first edition), chapter 51

Chapter Three

1. "Sifu" is a Chinese term that bears the dual meaning of "master" and "father." It is a term of respect and affection used when addressing one's teacher.

2. Awa Kenzo, Zen Bow, Zen Arrow by John Stevens, Shambhala Publications 2007

Chapter Four

1. It seems that the principles of music, once so clearly defined (perhaps overly so), have been up for debate in more recent times. The American composer John Cage, for example, wrote experimental pieces that consisted of the musicians playing *nothing at all* on their instruments for the duration of the piece, suggesting that the ambient sounds in the room can still be thought of as music. Maybe so. I'm not to say what the principles of music are or aren't. But I am suggesting that we need to know and align with the principles of an art form if we want to embody it.

2. The four stages of competence is a well-known psychological model that outlines the progression from incompetence to competence undergone by someone who learns a new skill, such as learning to drive or to speak a language. The four states are:

   1. Unconscious incompetence; we do not know that we do not know a thing. We may not even be aware of it as a possibility, or recognise it as a skill that can be learned.

   2. Conscious incompetence: we know that we do not know a thing. We have become aware, through having it pointed out to us, or through beginning the process of learning it, that our abilities are lacking.

   3. Conscious competence: we know that we know a thing. Through practice we have become skilled, but must maintain concentration and effort in order to perform the task or procedure.

   4. Unconscious competence: we do not know that we know a thing. We have become so practiced that it has become second nature, and we can perform it without conscious effort.

Chapter Five

1. "Ambalatthika-rahulovada Sutta: Instructions to Rahula at Mango Stone" (MN 61), translated from the Pali by Thanissaro Bhikkhu. Access to Insight (Legacy Edition), 30 November 2013, http://www.accesstoinsight.org/tipitaka/mn/mn.061.than.html

2. For further details see Majjhima Nikaya 58, "Abhaya Sutta: To Prince Abhaya"

3. A treatment of how and why it may be that intoxication by psychoactive substances and electronic media are treated so differently in our society is far beyond the scope of this book; for those who are interested, the author and visionary Terence McKenna has some interesting things to say in his book 'Food of the Gods.'

Chapter Six

1. The Dhammapada: The Path of Truth, Translated by the venerable Balangoda Ananda Maitreya 1995

2. Ajahn Chah was a greatly influential meditation master in the Thai forest tradition of Buddhism. He died in the early nineties, but not before he'd thoroughly instructed a number of Western disciples who went on to promulgate his direct and down-to-earth style of meditation and his profound and accessible teachings to a generation of explorers eager to imbibe wisdom. It is these offerings that facilitated my own stumbling odyssey along the deep and ancient path of meditation.

Chapter Seven

1. A Dhammapada for Contemplation, Ch.144 – A rendering by Ajahn Munindo

2. Morihei Uyeshiba, The Art of Peace by John Stevens, Shambhala Publications 2002

3. Ibid

4. Awa Kenzo, Zen Bow, Zen Arrow by John Stevens, Shambhala Publications 2007

Chapter Eight

1. There are various transliterations of the Chinese name "wing chun;" often the spelling denotes a particular lineage of the art. The lineage I belong to uses the spelling "wing tsun;" however, for the sake of ease I have opted throughout this book to use the more common and well-known spelling.

2. Bodhidharma is thus considered not only the 28th patriarch of Zen, but the first patriarch of Zen in China.

3. The Zen teachings of Bodhidharma (from The Bloodstream Sermon), Translated by Red Pine, published by North Point Press, a division of Farrar, Straus and Giroux, 1989.

4. Ibid.

5. Ibid.

6. Lao Tsu, Tao Te Ching, ch. 61.

7. Ibid, ch. 43. This particular aphorism I commissioned a local calligraphy master to render on a scroll as a gift to my sifu, so representative of his teaching do I feel it to be. The aphorism continues with the lines: "Silence and inactivity: very few understand them."

8. Ibid, ch.76.

9. "Loy lau hoy song" is the rough transliteration from Cantonese. This is the first half of the maxim, and is followed by "lut sau jik chong," which means "on loss of contact, thrust the hand forward."

10. Morihei Uyeshiba, The Art of Peace by John Stevens, Shambhala Publications 2002

Chapter Nine

1. Dhamma is a Pali word (Dharma in Sanskrit) conveying a variety of meanings, including the immutable way of nature, the teaching of the Buddha, and any thing, object, or event. In this context it carries the specific meaning of the teaching of the Buddha. The discourse the Buddha gave to those five ascetics was the Dhammacakkappavattana Sutta, "The Discourse on Setting the Wheel of Dhamma in Motion."

2. Ariyapariyesana Sutta: The Noble Search, Majjhima Nikaya 26. This is my own rendering, cobbled together from several well-known translations.

3. John 14:6

4. That sage was Ramana Maharshi. His story is remarkable: as a youth he was one day gripped by a sudden terror of death. His response, far from distracting himself from the specter of death's awful presence, was to fall to the floor, rigid and unmoving in mimic of death's rigor mortis. Then he questioned: "The body is gone, what remains? The mind!" And, putting the workings of the mind aside he questioned further what remained in the absence of that. The answer impressed itself so clearly and powerfully that never again did identification with those cast off relics of body and mind arise. Later, after years of keeping total silence and at the persistent requests of others, he began to teach a method of self-inquiry.

5. Lao Tsu, Tao Te Ching, ch.16.

6. This is a quote from Zen master Shunryu Suzuki (Zen Mind, Beginner's Mind, Weatherhill 1970).

JEREMY COLE has worked over the years as a saddler, a jeweller, a musician, a homeopath and, most recently, a web developer. He began studying wing chun kung fu in 2006, and has been practicing meditation for the past twenty years, primarily within the Theravada Buddhist tradition. His first book *Divine Laziness: The Art of Living Effortlessly* won the 2017 Ashton Wylie Charitable Trust Literary Award. He lives on the coast in New Zealand, his homeland, with Kate and a flock of seagulls.